funeral

KT-216-322

22. JUN 13

24. OCT 08

It's your
funeral

Inspiring ideas for a personal send-off

Emma George

Editor Roni Jay

WHITE
LADDER
PRESS
new tricks for old dogs

Published by White Ladder Press Ltd

Great Ambrook, Near Ipplepen, Devon TQ12 5UL

01803 813343

www.whiteladderpress.com

First published in Great Britain in 2008

10 9 8 7 6 5 4 3 2 1

13-digit ISBN 978 1 905410 27 9

British Library Cataloguing in Publication Data

A CIP record for this book can be obtained from the British Library.

Designed and typeset by Julie Martin Ltd
Cover design by Julie Martin Ltd
Printed and bound by TJ International Ltd, Padstow, Cornwall
Cover printed by St Austell Printing Company
Printed on totally chlorine-free paper
The paper used for the text pages of this book is FSC certified.
FSC (The Forest Stewardship Council) is an international
network to promote responsible management of the world's forests.

FSC
Mixed Sources
Product group from well-managed
forests and other controlled sources

Cert no. SGS-COC-2482
www.fsc.org
© 1996 Forest Stewardship Council

 White Ladder books are distributed in the UK by Virgin Books

White Ladder Press
Great Ambrook, Near Ipplepen, Devon TQ12 5UL
01803 813343
www.whiteladderpress.com

Love infinity plus one to Andrew, Zach and Daisy

For Bill Harrison 1913-1996

Contents

O how shall I warble myself for the dead one there I loved?

And how shall I deck my song for the large sweet soul that
   has gone?

And what shall my perfume be, for the grave of him I love?

Sea-winds, blown from east and west,

Blown from the eastern sea and blown from the western sea,
   till there on the prairies meeting:

These, and with these, and the breath of my chant,

I'll perfume the grave of him I love.

Walt Whitman

from *When Lilacs Last in the Door-yard Bloom'd*

Acknowledgements

As a child I used to lie awake trying to grasp the concept of eternity. When you die it's forever and ever and ever ... I used to whisper it over and over again, it just seemed unfathomable.

This journey began, like so many, on an impulse, with a question. Maybe it began way back then, when I realised forever didn't include me. I wanted to know about death, I wanted to know why no one else seemed to want to, why our inevitable end is so feared, so hidden, so unmentioned.

Like all curious fools I set off with the knowledge that if you're lucky you will meet the people who can offer you wisdom and open your mind. If you're really lucky you will find yourself in The Zone – that place of synchronicity, possibility and even the Truth. Or if not the Truth at least some interesting takes on it.

A couple of summers ago I met Josefine Speyer, co-founder, with her husband Nicholas Albery, of the Natural Death Centre, in the rather surreal setting of the Cremation Society annual conference. We talked about life, death and funerals and she asked me why I was there. I was actually writing an article on alternatives to cremation at the time, but Josefine looked at me with her bright intelligent eyes and said that maybe unconsciously there was another reason, that there was something in this I needed, maybe to come to terms with my own mortality.

When I tell people I'm writing about funerals they slowly begin to back away, but often they pause, they ask a question. Most people have been to a dreadful funeral and never forgotten it; some have been to an amazing funeral and never forgotten it. We carry these experiences with us, as we carry the memories of our dead, as we inherit their gestures, their ideas, the reflections of them that are woven into our own complicated histories.

This book is about how to make funerals better, to provide a little knowledge and understanding, some inspiration and encouragement, because we need to, not out of dread or duty, but out of love.

Most of this I owe to Rupert and Claire Callender, of the Green Funeral Company in Cornwall who one quiet day kicked me into the Zone and have been doing so ever since, and I have the scars to prove it. We can be esoteric about all this, but it's the people at the coalface who can really teach us. When I met Fred Christophers, the undertaker, of Ashburton, he was fixing a wall. I joked about him doing a bit of DIY and he rounded on me, informing me that he had been a builder all his life. I stood corrected, and I thank him for sharing with me his experience of half a century of attending to the dead.

Likewise the Rev'd Fr Frederick Denman, the vicar of Sparkwell, near Plymouth, was happy to tell me about his experience in taking funerals. Frederick is the kind of priest that really makes you think getting up early on Sunday morning and standing in a very old and draughty building could actually be a good idea.

Also Thomas Lynch, with one foot in Michigan and one in County Clare, poet and undertaker, who I thank for allowing me to use his words, snatched before a poetry reading a couple of autumns ago.

My thanks also go to Roni Jay, Mike Jarvis, John Bradfield (adviser for the AB Welfare & Wildlife Trust for information on the relevant law) the staff at Torquay crematorium, Sue Gill and John Fox, Jane Morell and Simon Smith, and Peter Rock at Ecopod. Also to Spider, Mark Arnold, Valerie Brown, Jan O'Highway, Sarah and all the family and friends who were very patient indeed.

I am particularly grateful to those good people who entrusted me with their own experiences of loss, and hope it informs and comforts you in yours.

Extract acknowledgements

Extract from *The Dead Good Funeral Guide* by Sue Gill and John Fox reprinted with kind permission from Dead Good Books.

Extracts from *The Undertaking* by Thomas Lynch reprinted with kind permission from Vintage, Random House Group Ltd.

Extracts from *How We Die* by Sherwin B Nuland reprinted with kind permission from Vintage, Random House.

Disclaimer

This information contained in this book is intended for advice and information only. It is recommended that professional legal advice be sought where necessary. Neither the publisher, the author, nor AB Welfare and Wildlife Trust can be held responsible for any errors or misleading statements on any point of law which may appear in this book.

Foreword

The first few numbing days of grief, those hours out of time between someone we love dying and their funeral, is just the beginning. The effects of losing someone can last a lifetime.

Doing the right thing requires courage and imagination. It is entirely possible to do it on automatic; to reach for the Yellow Pages while cocooned with shock, to let a funeral director and a priest you've never met explain the etiquette – the complicated table manners of bereavement (largely based on not frightening or embarrassing anybody else). You can then watch the ritual safe from the audience, and take your chances with the unresolved. It is tempting. I have done it myself. Or you can take the difficult path, which this book is all about.

As a society we are changing rapidly. Our sacred is running into our secular and funerals are not as simple as they once were. This book reflects this. It is not impartial or even-handed. It's not a *Which?*guide, and there are many other ways a funeral can be experienced in Britain today. But Emma has a position, and this book presents it.

If these things happen to you, or rather when these things happen to you, have courage. Slow down. Tell the truth, mention the unmentionable – talk about love. Cry if you can, but also remember it's OK to laugh. Get this into everyone's head, and everyone's heart. Feel it while it's happening. Remember that what you do now is responsible for how you will feel about love and loss forever.

Jump.

Rupert Callender
Director, The Green Funeral Company

Introduction

A few mourners in a church, it's a suburban church, no grandeur, just a lot of Formica and some pink carnations. The mourners have never been here before, the dead man only came here for the funerals of his friends. The vicar talks about him, a few minutes, a bare synopsis of a man who was loved, a man who is no more. The coffin is taken to the crematorium, the mourners shuffle. They are wearing formal clothes in a formal place and are unsure of what to do or what to say. It is a closed coffin, and there is a grim finality as it disappears. There is nothing left of the man, some ashes placed in the garden of remembrance. The mourners eat sausage rolls in a hall and look at old photographs and feel empty and lost.

This was my grandfather's funeral. The great smiling, hugging, chocolate-bearing, story-telling hero of my childhood, and adulthood too, gone. All I can really remember ten years later is the numbness, the feeling that this wasn't enough. My grandfather is nowhere. I don't have anywhere to visit him, the memory or idea of him. The garden of remembrance at Salisbury Crematorium – is that it?

When my great-grandfather died my brother and I didn't go to the funeral; it wasn't deemed appropriate for children. I was protected against the nasty inevitability of my mortality and consigned to fearful, restless nights on my own, wondering.

The truth is I never said goodbye to my grandfather. I was abroad when he died and, ten years on, there is an aching, a sadness. This is not an unusual story, and I've spoken to many people who have had similar experiences.

There is a real temptation to sleepwalk your way through the funeral. You turn up on the day and think when you've got through it, when it's over, that's half the battle done, and it absolutely is not. Shock is a wonderful thing, it insulates people in a fantastic way but you have to know how to use it and not get numbed by it. My father died when I was seven and my mother died when I was 25, and I didn't handle those funerals very well. I didn't go to my father's funeral and I can't remember anything about my mother's, what coffin she had, I can't remember what hymns we sang, what anyone said, and it wore me down for years.

Rupert Callender

Notes on Diana

My son was born early in the morning after Diana died, he was born in water, at home. We were in this little bubble of awe and wonder, surrounded by flowers with our beautiful baby, aware of this grief, this mourning all around, it was very strange. It was as though we were on one axis of love, while the nation was on the other.

With Diana we saw this mass mourning, people were mourning not only Diana, but the aunts, uncles, fathers, mothers, brothers and sisters we never got a chance to grieve for.

Thomas Lynch

Diana died less than a year after my mother and it really helped me. I got up at 6am on the day of the funeral, with the rest of the nation, and I watched the whole thing, and I wept and wept and wept. It does annoy me when people say, 'Oh, this dreadful culture where you mourn people you haven't met,' but really we were all crying for the ones we lost.

Rupert Callender

Live well and prepare to die

'Take Care, Live Well and Prepare to Die'–

from a gravestone, in Dartington, Devon

It was the Victorians who formalised our funerals and created these lavish affairs, with horse-drawn hearses adorned with ostrich plumes, mourners in black, and elaborate coffins. It was the Victorians who carved the names of their dead in stone.

When somebody died, the clocks were literally stopped, the curtains drawn, and mirrors covered, black mourning clothes were worn, for weeks or months or years. Victoria never came out of mourning for Albert.

The Victorians knew death, it was all around, life expectancy was 40 and three out of every 20 babies died. Death couldn't be ignored or hidden, but was considered something to be prepared for and expected. Children were told stories about it.

Degrees of separation

The degrees of separation between the dead and the living have steadily increased. Victorian mourning rituals were not appropriate in the face of world war and the loss of life on such a vast scale. Funerals became the domain of the funeral director and not the family. Before that, people died at home and were laid out in the same room in which they had courted their lovers and birthed their children.

Modern medicine has doubled our lifespan in less than a hundred years and confined death more and more to the old. In the last fifty years dying has became institutionalised and is now the realm of the doctors and the hospitals rather than the family. Today, there are more degrees of separation between the living and the dead. The dead are someone else's responsibility. If we see them at all they are in a funeral home, 'prepared for a viewing'.

Our families these days are so fractured, we often live far away from our beginnings, away from our parents, who spend their last years in sheltered housing, care homes, retirement complexes. Death, like the family, has become someone else's problem and for the most part hidden from our lives.

I was in Ireland in April 2005 when Pope John Paul II died. I was impressed by the fact so many people went to see him. Four million people went to Rome. They were not going to see the architecture of the city, they were going to see the body of the dead Pope. You hear people in America or Britain saying how very Catholic, how very Italian, how very Polish, when in fact it's very human. And it's been done by humans all the way through-

> *out history right up until the last 40 years. For 40,000 years the living have dealt with their dead in their bodies, not in the idea of the thing but the thing itself. Only in the past 40 years have we vanquished the dead from their own funerals. Everyone's invited but the dead guy.*
>
> Thomas Lynch

The art of dying

A Good Death, according to the church, was one where the dying would patiently hold a crucifix, in the presence of a cleric. The person was not to be given hope of recovery by those around him, nor talk to him of material possessions, to distract from his spiritual ascent. A beautiful death was something to strive for.

These secular days a good death often means a death without pain, a death with dignity. Sherwin B Nuland, a surgeon, writes in his book *How We Die* about how these expectations are in conflict with modern medicine which, 'Is all too frequently a series of destructive events that involve by their very nature the disintegration of the dying person's humanity'.

It's so hard to let them go, our people, our blood, our loves, and so often they go in hospitals, under harsh lighting, connected to tubes, medicated and confused. Nuland talks about how the art of saving life has replaced the art of dying.

"Modern dying takes place in the modern hospital, where it can be hidden, cleansed of its organic blight and finally packaged for modern burial. We can now not only deny the power of death, but of nature itself."

Sherwin B Nuland

"Death is a natural part of life – it's not an illness. It's very important for the medical profession to recognise when a person is dying. There is a point when there is a transition; this is now a dying time, there is no use in trying to work with emergency measures to keep this person alive. We must recognise this person is dying and other things have to come in. We have to support this person in their spiritual journey of letting go and dying, and it involves not only the person who is dying, but also the people they are closest to."

Josefine Speyer

The natural death movement

"The living can do a great deal to make the passage easier for the dying, to raise the most purely physiological act of human existence to the level of awareness or even spirituality."

Aldous Huxley

In the 1970s the natural birth movement reclaimed birth, successfully campaigning for women to have their babies at home as a natural process, rather than in hospital as a medical one. Today the natural death movement is trying to reclaim death, to give the dying the choice of how they would like to die and whether they would like to stay at home.

New models of a Good Death have been achieved by the hospice movement, and pioneers and mavericks like Dr Keri Thomas who worked with Macmillan Cancer Relief, and Nicholas Albery and Josefine Speyer who founded the Natural Death Centre in 1991. Nicholas Albery, writer, social inventor and human dynamo, had witnessed the natural birth of his son and asked: "Wouldn't more people, if it were possible, prefer to die at home amongst friends rather than in the anonymity of a big and noisy hospital? As with birth could preparation exercises and rituals help reduce the anxieties that people feel about dying? Could dying at least for the lucky few become as easy and ecstatic as our experience of birth?"

As well as advising the dying and their carers, the Natural Death Centre has for over 15 years been advising families who want to arrange a funeral themselves.

Everything's gone green

As we lurch towards some awareness of the havoc we have been wreaking on our planet, natural burials in woodland or meadows are no longer the preserve of the new age, to the sound of gentle drum beats and the fragrance of patchouli, and the subject of wry articles in the Sunday supplements. Instead, green funerals have become acceptable as a real alternative to traditional funerals. There is now a huge range of biodegradable coffins available and more than 200 woodland burial sites.

When formality is needed

> *Someone has died in my town, a young man, 30 years old, there is a huge gathering of his peers. They file slowly into the church, predominantly dressed in black. The funeral procession arrives, the hearse is sleek, immaculate, the bearers solemnly carry the coffin, a wooden casket, with a wreath in the shape of a football on the top, everything is slow motion, the sound drains from the street. There's a formality framing this inevitability, a structure – this is how funerals are. The door closes on the church.*

When we face tragedy, sometimes the framework, the one we know, is the one that we need. We need the grandness of the church, we need the presence of a god, whatever our beliefs. We need to wear black and mourn our loss. No two funerals are the same, because no two people are the same. A funeral is whatever you need to get to the next stage.

So this book is not about getting everybody to anoint their dead with oils and take to the streets with candlelight and samba bands. It's really about choice, about how we say good-bye to our people. It's about looking at these questions and delving deep inside ourselves to find the answers.

If you lose someone then this process may be incredibly painful and difficult, but liberation comes with choice, and in the rollercoaster of emotions that is the aftermath of a death, a good funeral will provide solace now and later.

It's about how we let them go.

> *"If you give people freedom to express themselves they will usually rise to it. You see the light shining out of their eyes, and the enormous wells of courage and strength among friends and families, and a real sense of community."*
>
> Rupert Callender

CHAPTER 1

Someone has died

> "Oh Lord, give each of us his own death."
>
> Rainer Maria Rilke
> Austro-German poet, d.1926

This chapter addresses the beginning of the ending. It's not designed to overload your mind but to give you the absolutes on what must be done. It also contains a collection of ideas and thoughts to consider over the first day or two.

Don't bolt the funeral

> "Most people don't think about the funeral until after the death, then they panic and think that there's a bureaucratic stream of events that has to happen. They also presume that the body does outrageous things really quickly, neither of which is true. So, the tendency is to bolt the funeral and end up with this event that

> *doesn't reflect the person that has died at all. You need time to work out what you need, what will work for everyone."*
>
> Rupert Callender

> *"From my point of view I think that organising the funeral was an incredibly useful displacement activity. As an ex-stage manager I wasn't daunted, and I had a huge amount of help of course, and it allowed me to keep my mind occupied but still focused on Rich. This was a blessing at a time when I really hardly knew what I was doing."*
>
> from Roni's story [see Chapter 4]

Funeral myths

∗ You have to have a funeral

∗ You have to be in a licensed building

∗ You have to use a clergyman, an undertaker, and a coffin

∗ You have to use a public burial ground

There are very surprisingly few rules when someone dies. In fact there are more rules for a farmer when a sheep dies. There are so many myths about funerals because of our reluctance as a society to think about them other than as a grim inevitability, and it is in the interests of the funeral profession to perpetuate these myths. They are very lucrative.

The Three Absolutes

There are very few things you must do when a person dies.

You must:

1 Obtain a medical Cause of Death certificate

2 Register the fact that a death has occurred

3 Dispose of the body by burial or cremation following the correct procedure

When you must do them

∗ You should obtain the medical Cause of Death certificate from a doctor (or two if cremation is going to take place), as soon as the person has died.

∗ You should register the death with your local registrar within five days of the death (unless the coroner is involved, or you are unable to for another reason).

∗ The cremation or burial can be days or weeks after the death.

[See Forms and Formalities, Chapter 9]

What is a funeral?

We die. And we've been trying to make sense of it forever: our religions, our rituals, our gods, our myths. Neanderthal skeletons were discovered with a layer of pollen in their burial chambers. In some cultures funeral rituals are elaborate, some are very simple, some people wail and weep and rail against mortality, other cultures see the soul as eternal, and bless its journey into the next incarnation.

A good funeral

"No two people are the same, so no two funerals are the same. A good funeral should fulfill the wishes of the deceased and provide an opportunity for the bereaved, family and friends to join together to celebrate the life of that person."

Mike Jarvis, Director, Natural Death Centre

"The most important thing for us is helping the family arrange a funeral appropriate to the person that has died, whether it's a samba band processing through a wood by candlelight or four people standing in silence around a grave."

Claire Callender

"A funeral should be specific to the person, the site, the season.

The context should be relevant and distinctive, and have meaning for those taking part. A funeral should be a strong ending of one chapter and the marking of the beginning of a new chapter. It is about the end of a life with them and the beginning of a life without them."

Sue Gill, co-author, The Dead Good Funerals Book (2004)

"A good funeral should be personal and authentic and relate to the person who has died so that it reflects their beliefs and life story."

Simon Smith, Green Fuse funeral organisers, Devon

Maybe the person who died knew exactly what they wanted, maybe you discussed it together, maybe they left a letter, told a friend, maybe you'd laughed about it late one night when you felt you would live forever. Maybe you never had time. Gather those threads that you are left with and gather those people closest and begin.

Key decisions to make

✳ Do you know the wishes of the person who has died?

✳ Will you be using the professionals or doing it yourself?

✳ Is there a funeral director you know?

✳ Do you want a burial or a cremation?

✳ If you choose a burial, will it be in a cemetery, woodland or private ground?

✳ Will the service be religious or secular?

✳ How involved do you want to be?

✳ Are you planning a memorial such as scattering the ashes?

There's no bullshit around death

Family dynamics are so complicated, we weave these intricate webs, we leave things undone, sometimes we leave things broken, and that's the way it is. Sometimes death can be a catalyst, sometimes it can be a release, it can be a time of reconciliation, or forgiveness, or regret or recrimination.

Whatever it is, hold on.

As Claire Callender says, "Death exposes fault lines, stuff that has been suppressed for 30 or 40 years. People can keep up appearances at a wedding, but around death there's a lot of emotional honesty. For us, that week or ten days leading up to the funeral is the most important part of our work, it makes up 70 or 80 percent of what we do. We get involved with the family emotionally and take them through a different process. In a way we take a bit of the priest's role. The actual funeral is just the coming together and the crystallisation of this work."

> *"Families are so complicated, and it's so important to communicate honestly. I wish we'd all had a chance to sit down and plan the funeral together. He was my dad too, and I was left with this terrible empty feeling for so long afterwards."*
>
> from Susannah's story [see Chapter 5]

Find your lieutenant

Claire Callender advises that when someone dies it's not just about what one person needs. She says, "There are usually three generations of family and friends around, so a huge part of our job is negotiating with factions of a family who want different things. We work with them until we find something that works for everyone.

"When a young person dies and there is going to be a big funeral, there is always an organised family friend who knows everyone, and they are your lieutenant. In a funeral like this a big part of the job is to set up and facilitate, so we start delegating: who will organise chairs for the reception, who will organise the music, and usually there's this really committed, lovely, person to work with.

"We have seen people who have been through this terrible tragedy and they would open the door and someone would just collapse on them and need supporting for an hour, until they go on their way, and another one arrives. Somehow we've lost that gesture of turning up with a casserole – that really helps. It's about empathising and not just wringing your hands."

This is where your lieutenant comes in. At a funeral the bereaved person should not spend the day looking after people less upset than they are.

> *"Shock is one of the most useful of all our self-protecting instincts and gets undeserved bad press. The flip side to its usefulness is a tendency to paralyse. Somebody in shock needs such delicate handling; so much information is unabsorbed and of course this is a time when many decisions need to be made. People tend to think that shock is a short-term condition lasting days at the most. In fact the effects of shock can still be felt months, even years later. It is both hallucinatory and deadening. It can confuse you into thinking you don't care, that you don't love the person you've just lost. There is of course a strong comic aspect to this seemingly invincible state. You need to be assured this is OK, you need to be told your reactions are normal, useful and don't reflect the truth of your relationship."*
>
> Rupert Callender

CHAPTER 2

Looking after the body

> "The bodies of the newly dead are not debris or remnant, nor are they entirely icon or essence. They are, rather, changelings, incubates, hatchlings of a new reality that bear our names and dates, our image and likeness, as surely in the eyes and ears of our children and grandchildren as did word of our birth in the ears of our parents and grandparents. It is wise to treat such new things carefully, tenderly, with honour."
>
> Thomas Lynch, The Undertaking

This chapter is about the actuality of the person who died and some thoughts on where the body should be before the funeral, with some wisdom and experience to help you decide.

When somebody dies the body can be kept at home or in a Chapel of Rest, or at a mortuary or funeral home. It is possible to store the body with a funeral director even if you are not using any of their other services, until the funeral or the day before. If the person died in a hospital you can take them home. A funeral director will arrange this or you can do it yourself.

There is so much distance between the living and the dead, many of us do not experience death in our inner circles until our middle ages; many of us have never seen a dead body. So often the dead are removed from our lives, hidden, the reality of them denied in this painful transition from a reality to a memory.

How we used to die

Up until about 1960 when someone died it would usually be at home. Someone would inform the family doctor, who would come and certify the death. The 'layer out' would be called, the woman who would attend our births and deaths, our comings and goings. Every village or street would have one. The women in the family would help to wash and dress the person and attend to their last offices.

The undertaker was usually the local builder who had simply added 'undertaker' to his duties. He would call and pay his respects, take the measurements and make the coffin from sets of oak, mahogany or elm, only sleeping when it was done. The next morning, the person would be put in their coffin and laid out in their nightclothes or Sunday best.

A small altar would be placed at the foot of the coffin, candles and fragrant flowers placed around and the family would sit with the body, laugh, cry, and tell stories. Neighbours and friends would visit and pay their respects.

After three or four days the coffin would be carried or driven to church, sometimes carried past places significant to the deceased. People would stand outside their houses, out of respect, and be reminded that life is indeed transitory.

Spending time with the body

"The setting was perfect and just what Rich would have liked, and we all went in to see his body, apart from one of my boys who chose to see the coffin after the lid was on. It was so peaceful, with no sound but the birdsong, that we were all really pleased we had decided to see him."

from Roni's story

Claire Callender emphasises that they would never force people to see the body, but they do encourage it. She says, "People come here and they're incredibly nervous, and we give them a cup of tea, and then take them out to our Chapel of Rest, which is a beautiful old building near the river. They might stay ten minutes or half an hour, but when they come back there's an obvious change in them. Their faces are relaxed and their eyes are clear – it's quite magical. You can see that there is a little bit more acceptance of the situation."

It may for many reasons be impossible, impractical or too disturbing to be with the body. There are manifold reasons why a death can be violent, or intrusive. It may be that the memory of that person, living, present, vital, is the one you want to hold with you. One does not necessarily cancel out the other.

> *"You shouldn't stop someone seeing a body if it is a violent death. They know that it's been violent, and if they don't see the body, then they never stop imagining it. Never. If a mother has lost a child in a terrible way, it's her instinct to hold that child, to examine that child, look after that child. People react against that, but how can it be wrong?"*
>
> Rupert Callender

Chapels of Rest

Rupert Callender feels strongly about these. "Most Chapels of Rest are a disgrace – tiny spaces, curtains at the back, with fake flowers and a strong smell of air freshener, and no windows.

None of them have a space where you think, 'I could sit here for hours'." Rupert's partner Claire adds, "We did a funeral for a teenager. All his friends came down before the funeral and the Chapel of Rest was full of champagne bottles, overflowing ashtrays, the CD was still playing and you think, 'That's how it should be'."

Laying out the body

Laying out the body means washing and dressing it. This can be done by a district nurse, a funeral director or the family [for details see Forms and Formalities on page 147]. For Muslims the family wash and dress the body as part of the funeral ritual. It is seen for some as a last act of caring, for others it may be just too much.

> *"If this is what you want to do, you don't have to do it all by yourself. You can get the community nurse to help you. You may just comb their hair; that in itself is a huge step, you stay connected in some way."*
>
> Sue Gill

Dress me in McQueen

A friend of mine wants to be dressed in Alexander McQueen.

If the person died in hospital they will be dressed in a hospital gown; an undertaker may dress them in a shroud. These can look quite spooky but you can dress them in anything. However for cremation and natural burial, natural fabric is kindest. For cremation there must not be any jewellery or metal.

Ritual

Being in the presence of the body of someone you loved can be a very powerful and moving experience. The hours and days after a death can be a time of peace, understanding, coming together – the beginning of the letting go. Family and friends may gather to tell stories, raise a glass, or just sit with the person. You can light incense, sing, pray, or anoint the person with oils.

Sitting with the body overnight is a powerful ritual occurring in many cultures. Symbolically it is to bid the soul 'a good journey'.

"Bringing the body home for an overnight vigil before the funeral can be useful," says Claire Callender, "especially funerals for the young. Teenagers usually know something like 200 people, all of whom have to come to terms with the death. So seeing the body really helps them. It's a massive thing for the family to do, to open their house to traumatised teenagers, but it can be amazing too.

"If it's a child under ten that has died they have usually been ill and an intense amount of caring will have been involved, so when they die not only is there a space where the child was, but that routine of caring has just stopped. If you bring the body home, there's still some caring that has to be done: you have to change the ice packs, you can tuck them up. After a few days the family will be ready to let them go to the next stage, and this process happens naturally over the course of a few days, rather than snatch, in the fridge, then in the coffin and the next time you see them is at the graveside."

Body changes

The human body devoid of life changes rapidly, the skin becomes sallow and waxy very quickly. Stiffness, due to the build up of lactic acid on the no longer working muscles, sets in after a few hours and comes and goes. Unless it is kept in a mortuary, the body will start to deteriorate and smell after two or three days. The body devoid of life may still release fluids. It is a good idea to have advice and support from someone experienced.

Embalming

This controversial process was until recently carried out routinely when preparing a body for burial or cremation. Embalming is essentially a process that makes the person look as if they are not dead. It is about preservation and presentation, replacing the blood with formaldehyde (or there is now a biodegradable fluid) and restoring their face and body to an illusion of 'health'. The environmental cost of embalming is high: it forces noxious chemicals into the earth or air. Natural burial grounds often do not allow embalmed bodies.

Embalming is necessary if the funeral cannot take place for more than two weeks, for instance if an important mourner is abroad and can't get back sooner. Some cancers make the body deteriorate very quickly, and in this case embalming is also recommended.

Rupert Callender tells of a man who had died of cancer at the age of 42. When his body was prepared, he wasn't embalmed. His father-in-law came to see him, having once seen his own father after embalming. Rupert says, "He had found it eerie. Seeing his son-in-law was very different. Although he was gaunt, and looked ill, it seemed natural and he felt more peaceful."

"We feel as though our whole job is to help people come to terms with the fact that this person has died, not take them to see them when they look like they've just come back from holiday and they're having a bit of a nap."

Claire Callender

Jim and Margaret's funeral – Mark's story

Mum and Dad both passed away in 2005; they were both in their 80s. We had always talked about death very openly, partly because my sister had died very unexpectedly twenty years earlier. I'd given them the Natural Death Handbook and they'd both read the relevant parts. The good thing about talking about death with those who are approaching it is that you can discuss their wishes, rather than just write them down.

Mum and Dad were very much of the cremation line initially, but at that time I was becoming greener and greener and was concerned about cremation as not being at all eco-friendly. So we talked about a greener route and they were happy with a green burial. We also touched on coffins and they said that they would be happy with a cardboard coffin or a home-made coffin.

They died within a couple of years of talking about it. Mum had a massive stroke and was unable to do anything herself but breathe. As soon as Dad realised that she wasn't going to be there with him any more, he declined very rapidly. The day he passed away, I had been with him in the morning and I knew he was going to go.

After the nursing home called to tell me I went straight back and told them I was going to take the body in a friend's vehicle. They were a little bit surprised, but said they wouldn't stop me. My friend had brought his van and we had some blankets. Because Dad had lost so much weight I could pick him up myself. I carried him out and laid him in the back of the van and we took him home.

I laid him out on a trestle table in his garden shed, which was one of his favourite spots, and I cleared it out and lit some candles and incense and arranged some nice flowers and put some of his favourite objects all around, pictures of Mum and his parents. It was amazing, being in his potting shed. There were only two places he really loved: his shed and his office.

I washed him, which was the most moving experience of

my life. To be that close to a loved one when they're dead is completely different to when they're alive; it was a very empowering moment. I'd had time to think about this before and I didn't want someone who didn't know my Dad to deal with his body. I treated him with as much care and delicacy as I would have if he was alive. There was no rigor mortis for about 24 hours, so it gave me a chance to move him around, but the next day when I dressed him his limbs were very rigid.

I wanted people to have a chance to see him and say their last goodbyes. My sister was in Canada, so it gave her a chance to fly over and pay her last respects. Meanwhile, Mum was in a home, and completely incapable. We knew she couldn't speak, we didn't know whether she could hear, but we felt it was her right to be close to him. So we organised an ambulance to bring her over. We carried her across the lawn, and laid her next to Dad and I put her hand in his hand. It was very emotional. I told her, "This is Daddy's hand." I don't know if she understood but I knew that this would be the last time they'd ever be together, and it was so important for the letting-go process.

All this was far more powerful than the funeral was, and

I suspected at the time I was doing so much grieving now, that the funeral would be just the final door. I put more plants in the room, more photographs, and we ordered a cardboard coffin. They sent us the right size coffin, but the wrong size chipboard slab which goes inside. This was no problem for me because I'm a wood worker, but I imagine for someone else it could be very distressing. The company were very apologetic though.

We assembled the coffin, and it literally was a cardboard box with the chipboard at the bottom. As a carpenter, I would say you do need extra support. We assembled the coffin at my home and it gave us a chance to decorate it so the grandchildren helped and we all drew pictures and flowers and wrote little messages to Daddy and Grandpa.

Dad was never much of a churchgoer so we decided not to have a church service but to hold a ceremony here in the courtyard, which would be followed by a burial. My neighbour, a farmer, had kindly agreed to let us have a little plot of land a few hundred yards up the hill, looking over the whole valley. I knew what I had to do legally. I already had the landowner's permission and I had checked that it wasn't near a water-course. I would make a note on the deeds and notify the registrar.

I went to the field and decided I wanted Dad to be facing east to west, his feet facing towards the west. I dug the hole by hand; it's incredibly shaly land, and after the first 12 inches it was just compacted slate so it was a pickaxe job, breaking a bit and shoveling a bit, breaking a bit and shoveling a bit. I spent four hours one morning then about the same the next day. It's all part of the healing process, all part of the letting go and saying goodbye. Every little bit of soil you move is part of that ritual.

At one point someone brought me a picnic lunch and I sat at the edge of the hole with my legs dangling over. It was a balmy March day and I suddenly noticed the skylarks singing. I'd never noticed them this early and it was very touching. All these moments were incredibly poignant and I know I'll take them to my own grave.

I even lay in the bottom of the hole just to make sure it was big enough. I did it all by eye, it was a good straight hole. There's no law about how deep you have to dig. Some people say 30 inches, just enough so an animal can't dig it up. I wanted to go to six feet, symbolically it seemed right, but I think I got to about five-and-a-half.

We tested the coffin; it was a bit tight, but cardboard's

very forgiving, my advice would be to keep some tools handy, just in case. When I finished digging, I laid a green blanket over the grave and put a few flowers around and about and mowed the grass so it was a nice area for people to come in to.

Then we organised the service. My sister decided on the Order of Service and had it printed. She got in touch with people and arranged for donations to go to St Luke's Hospice in Plymouth, and we organised the wake.

About 60 or 70 people came to Dad's funeral; it was about a week after he had died. His coffin was laid out in the courtyard and we borrowed an arc of seats from a marquee company to put around it. I'd organised a number of people to help me bear the coffin, it's only chipboard but you need at least six people, even though he was so light. I had also put some wooden braces under it.

Some relatives said a few words and my daughter read a poem. I'm not one for public speaking, even in this situation. I felt my involvement in the funeral was practical. It was a sunny, calm, March day, the service was lovely and pretty much everyone walked up to the field and we laid the coffin next to the grave. We stood for a few moments in silence, the skylarks were singing and we all listened to them. It was very moving.

Everyone commented on what a beautiful site it was and how lucky we were to have been given it. We lowered the coffin, using some seatbelts we had got from the scrapyard. I threw in the first handful of soil, and then invited everyone to throw a flower. Some people said something, a prayer, a goodbye. Then we started digging, just enough to cover the coffin.

Afterwards we all went for a buffet at a country house nearby, and it gave me a chance to thank people for coming in a more relaxed environment, I was just sad I didn't get a chance to speak to everybody who had come.

I have noticed before when I have been to funerals, especially my sister's, that I was grieving a lot at the funeral, weeping, but at Mum and Dad's, because I'd shed so many tears in the run-up, by the time they were going into the ground it wasn't so raw.

After doing this with Dad, I realised this was such a beautiful thing to do, like spending your final moments with somebody. I've lived close to Mum and Dad most of my life and had a very close relationship with them, especially after my sister died.

The next day I filled the grave and planted some roses and trees around it. We made a mound, so we know where it is. It's incredible how quickly nature takes over.

It was only six months later, in the November, that Mum died. It was such a release for her. Mum was much bigger than Dad, and she had been fed through a tube. Her body was very different to look after. It's amazing how the body still functions after death. *The Natural Death Handbook* helped us deal with these practicalities.

We laid her out in the shed as well. Both my sisters were out of the country when she died, but it was a cold November. At night, I put blocks of ice on her and some blankets to keep in the cold: she was laid out for nearly ten days. Both of my sisters washed and dressed her. It seemed right that the son had attended to the father, the sisters to the mother. There were masses of flowers in the shed; it looked so beautiful. We had her favourite radio station on and all her favourite things around her.

I made a coffin for Mum, because she was larger, and I didn't think we would get away easily with a cardboard coffin. It was touching because I made the coffin with the floorboards that she helped me pull up from one of the barns, and we painted the coffin with her favourite colour she'd painted her fence with, just two years earlier.

Mum was more of a churchgoer than Dad. She used to clean some of the churches, so we held the service at her favourite one. The church was full. A friend had recommended a lovely lady, a fantastic singer, who had told us that she loved to sing *Over the Rainbow*, which is from one of Mum's favourite films. It was lovely.

We hired a hearse for the drive from the church to the graveside. We were very careful with the bearers, and practised with heights so the shortest was at the front and the tallest at the back. We all convened at the courtyard and walked up to the field. The weather was so bad in the run-up to the funeral that I used a little mini-digger to dig the grave. It only took half an hour, but it wasn't so neat so I finished it off by hand. Like Dad's funeral, the weather was unexpectedly sunny and warm, but there were no skylarks in November.

Both funerals were on a Saturday, which was lovely because people didn't have to worry about taking time off work, and it meant that people were still around on Sunday.

The next day I filled in the grave with the bearers who knew Mum. Everything you do, every little thing is part of saying goodbye.

We had a lot of time to prepare for Mum and Dad's funeral, we'd talked about it, and it was no surprise when they died, but it's very different if it's sudden. It's so tragic, and doing it this way would be very difficult; I think you'd need to get someone to help you.

Once they had both gone, I looked into the memorial. Dad was Cornish, so I really wanted some Cornish granite. I wanted a big piece to make a bench. I checked all the quarries and the only piece I found that was suitable turned out to be Chinese. The quarryman told me it was more expensive to move the granite from Southampton docks to Devon, than shipping it from China to England. It's sad that stone that comes half way around the world is cheaper than stone from your own ground. It was transported down here and an inscription put on it. I left some room for myself. I want to be buried there too, next to them.

The monumental mason told me that embossed lettering lasts longer than lettering that's carved in, especially with granite, which is prone to freeze-thaw action, so we had lead letters put on it, which would last a couple of hundred years. After that if someone wants to use the stone for a lintel for their fireplace, that's fine. ✶

CHAPTER 3

Planning for a funeral

A death has its absolutes: we must decide what will happen to the actual body, for now our choices are burial or cremation – the earth or the fire. We must decide whether the body will be finally rested in a coffin or a shroud. And we must decide whom we will entrust with the practicalities of these final arrangements.

Using the pros

A funeral director is a man who can enter a house where death has occurred and take upon himself the whole responsibility of organising and equipping a funeral. He is a technical adviser, agent, contractor, master of ceremonies and custodian of the body of his client

from the official manual of Funeral Directing

"It's a calling – you're always on call. My mother was a farmer's daughter, which was 365 days a year, my father was an undertaker, which was 365 days a year. You have to live over the shop, sleep with one ear on the phone. We get calls on Christmas morning, Boxing Day, people depend on you. Our holidays are few and far between; a day's cricket at Taunton suits me.

Fred Christophers, undertaker

Fred Christophers' family have attended to Devon's dead since 1846. He started in the family business at the age of 14. Fred attributes the longevity of the family to hard work and, in his grandfather's case, cider. Now in his 52nd year as an undertaker, Fred has no intention of retiring. When he started working, people were still rested at home and every village had an undertaker who was probably also the carpenter.

In the past 40 years the undertaker has become the funeral director, no longer a tradesman but a professional offering a service, though still assuming responsibility for the body of the deceased and the arrangements for the funeral. The funeral director was traditionally rooted in the community. A respected figure, he was someone you could rely on to get up at 2am on a winter's night to attend to a death amongst his townsfolk. The funeral director was a man of integrity, to be respected and in possession of an air of mystique, he knew death after all. It was likely his sons and daughters would become funeral directors, and the family business was often the family home.

The funeral director's business was largely steady, busier at Christmas or during hot summers and cold winters. It was largely unregulated and there was no competition: one funeral director for the town. Then came the 1980s and big business, driven by profits and margins, swooped in like a magpie, gathering up all these little nests. The funeral business became corporate and today the Co-op and Dignity are the major players. Although 63 per cent of funeral directors are still independent, this number is dropping as people like Fred Christophers retire, are bought out or move on. In my town the local funeral director is actually the Co-op although it is called Perrin & Sons: the last Mr Perrin retired years ago.

But there are still many like Fred Christophers across the country doing it as they always have. They will continue politely to decline the cash on the table from the Co-op or Dignity and attend to the needs of their townsfolk, mourn the diminishing sense of community and wonder which son or daughter is going to continue The Work.

Fred Christophers has a typically empathetic approach to the families he works with. As he says, "If someone comes in to do arrangements, I don't pick up a pen and start writing. I think it's important to listen. I have as much time as people need." He meets his clients several times in the days between the death and the funeral. "The first call is when I remove the body and see the family. Then the family come to do the arrangements and see me again. When they go to the funeral they see me for the third time, and after the funeral when we do the 'Thanks' notices or deal with the cremated remains, they see me for the fourth time. So it's about continuity. With the bigger companies, you might see four different people.

> *"There is a space for humour. On the most fundamental level that's where we differ from most undertakers."*
>
> Claire Callender

> *"Good funeral directors care about what the family wants and put aside their own view of how it should be. They need to be safe in what they're doing but not so cautious that it makes them blinkered."*
>
> Simon Smith, Green Fuse

The cost of dying

There is often a worry that unscrupulous funeral homes capitalise on grief, and the idea that talking about money after a death is inappropriate. If you really loved the deceased surely you would give them a 'walnut rose' coffin, rather than (whisper) a *cardboard* coffin. I have heard stories that a funeral cortege has stopped on the way to the funeral refusing to go further until the relatives pay the whole cost of the funeral in advance. This is, of course, unacceptable.

＊ The cost of a funeral has risen 61% since 2000

＊ The average cost of a funeral with a burial is £3,307

＊ The average cost of a funeral with a cremation is £1,954

Get a quote

It is important to get itemised quotes as prices vary wildly, even for fixed costs like burial plots. This is a good job to delegate, and it is useful to have prices in writing.

> *"We got some quotes for a family in Winchester and the most expensive funeral director wanted £1,100 for a willow coffin, double what everyone else was charging. When we looked into it, it was owned by a venture capital company, so there is a pressure to make as much money as they can. The standard is going down in terms of giving people choice, and going up in terms of trying to sell people packages."*
>
> Simon Smith, Green Fuse

Paying for the funeral

Funeral expenses can be paid out of the estate of the dead person. Probate – the legalities of death – takes time, but money can be released on production of a death certificate for immediate expenses. If there are no resources and no money has been set aside, things can get pretty miserable. There are a few options if this is the case.

> *"We will always help anybody in any circumstance. If they come to us with no money at all, we will help. I buried one man: he had hanged himself, and he had only four pence in his pocket, that was all."*
>
> Fred Christophers

Inexpensive funerals

Members of the National Society of Allied and Independent Funeral Directors offer a 'basic funeral', conveying the body to a chapel of rest or elsewhere, a basic coffin, a gown, a visit, embalming and a hearse and one limousine with staff to supervise. Medical certificates, burial or crematorium fees and fees for the minister conducting the service are extra.

Many councils provide information on good value funeral directors, and some funeral directors offer a package for residents of certain districts.

If there is no money

The government's social fund offers helps for those who do not have enough money to pay for the funeral and are in receipt of state benefits. However, the applicant has to prove no one in the immediate family can pay.

[See Forms and Formalities, Chapter 9]

If no one makes arrangements

The local authority has a duty to bury or cremate someone when no other arrangements have been made. A respectful but basic funeral will be conducted.

Pre-paid funerals

Pre-paid funerals are huge in the US where three-quarters of the population pay for their funeral in advance, and it's become a fast-growing business in the UK. Payment plans have quite deservedly received some bad publicity. There are horror stories of companies going bust leaving relatives with no chance of retrieving the funds, or worse still one American company was just spending the money and burying the bodies in a mass grave. Today, payment plans are far more regulated.

Advantages of pre-paying

∗ It takes the expense and pressure off the family

∗ It means you can buy tomorrow's funeral 'at today's prices'

∗ People often choose simple funerals

Disadvantages of pre-paying

∗ Those left behind have very little opportunity to participate in the funeral arrangements, which can be fairly prescriptive and limited

Questions to ask

If you're considering a pre-paid funeral, here are some points to consider. What would happen if you:

∗ move away from the area?

∗ die out of the country?

∗ die before payments are completed?

And you need to check what the plan covers, such as the cost of cremation.

Choose a plan that is approved by the Financial Services Authority or affiliated to the National Association for Pre-Paid Funeral Plans. Some natural burial grounds offer an opportunity to buy a funeral in advance.

Alternatively, you can simply invest some money in a high interest account or joint account, accessible to the executors or next of kin, to use when the time comes. It is possible to buy a plot in a natural burial ground in advance, if this is your preferred option.

Doing it yourself

It is possible to organise a funeral entirely without using a funeral director. For some people, a DIY or family-organised funeral is achievable, acceptable and incredibly rewarding. Psychotherapists have found that people who have been hands-on in organising the funeral have benefited in the grieving process. The Natural Death Centre offers advice and resources for families wishing to do their own funerals.

DIY essentials

You will need courage, time, support, preparation, research and persistence. However, you can achieve a funeral that is personal, eco-friendly and inexpensive.

> *"Everyone who has got involved with arranging the funeral has said how helpful it has been in coming to terms with the loss, rather than sitting like a rabbit caught in the headlights on the sofa for three or four days waiting for the funeral."*
>
> Sue Gill

Doing the funeral yourself entails:

∗ laying out and preparing the body

∗ buying a coffin or a shroud

∗ taking care of the body until the funeral

∗ transporting the body to home or to a mortuary

∗ arranging the burial or cremation

∗ organising the service or ceremony

∗ arranging transport of the body to the burial ground or crematorium

> *"Some people that we talk to want to deal with everything themselves, but more often people want to be involved with some part of the funeral. They do not want to go to a funeral director who says 'leave everything to us'; they want someone who can be more a facilitator, someone who will do the things the family are unable to do or uncomfortable about doing, like picking up the body from the mortuary. There are more undertakers now who will do this, but not enough."*
>
> Mike Jarvis, Director, the Natural Death Centre

Claire Callender warns against taking on the whole project without serious consideration. "When you're emotionally deeply stressed, and you've lost someone you love who was a massive part of your life, do you really want to be thinking about what goes in the finger rolls? For some people, keeping busy is absolutely necessary, and we support people who want to do it all themselves, but very few people want to do the whole thing."

> *"It's all part of the healing process, it's all part of the letting go and saying goodbye, every little bit of soil you move is part of that ritual."*
>
> from Mark's story

Burial or cremation

The law does not seem to be absolutely certain that a body must be buried or cremated, but any other options are probably too obscure to consider here. Whether we return to the warm earth, our beginnings, or are consigned to the eternal flame, our bodies turned to ash, is sometimes a matter of instinct. One friend of mine is claustrophobic and couldn't bear the idea of being buried. Sometimes it is a matter of faith – for Hindus the fire is the only option, for the Muslim and Jewish faiths it is forbidden. Today, more and more people are considering the ecological impact of burial and cremation.

Traditional burial

The Victorians gave us the graveyards we know today, with their extravagant shrines and poetics, the crumbling effigies a reminder of our impermanence, the impermanence even of stone. From the 1830s burial in a cemetery was seen as a sign of status, evident in cemeteries as Highgate and Kensal Green.

Until Victorian times people were wrapped in cloth and buried with a wooden marker on the grave. Graves were not meant to be there for ever. There is usually a limit on the time a grave is undisturbed, such as 75 or 100 years. After that the grave can be re-used and the existing remains re-buried.

Everyone has a right to be buried in their local parish church-yard, but because so many of these are now full it is more likely that there will be space in the town cemetery. Although cemeteries usually have a place to conduct a service, the ceremony can be held wherever you choose. There may also be restrictions on the type of memorial you can use. If you had a mausoleum in mind, do check. The cost of a grave can vary from a few hundred to a few thousand pounds. It is usual that the plot includes space for two people to be buried.

Cremation

For thousands of years the Christian church, and the belief in resurrection, was against cremation. Maybe it seemed too close to the eternal fires of hell. Cremation was once viewed as a barbaric pagan ritual. Now 70 per cent of us in Britain are cremated and it is still considerably cheaper than burial. Only the Japanese cremate more, whereas for the predominately Catholic nations the cremation figure is almost negligible. One Catholic priest told me that cremation services are "anodyne and bland" in comparison with the ornate rituals, holy water and incense of the Catholic Church.

The Cremation Society was formed in 1874 by Sir Henry Thompson, surgeon to Queen Victoria, who regarded cremation as a hygienic, cost-effective and land-efficient method of disposal. Another advantage was that the mourners would be spared standing in the rain at the graveside.

In 1884 William Price, an 85 year old Welsh Druid, cremated the body of his baby son on a huge fire on a hilltop, causing a riot and his arrest. However, cremation gradually became accepted and its popularity increased from the 1940s.

Nevertheless, there are environmental concerns about the amount of gas consumed in cremation. Cremators reach temperatures of 1000° C and the process takes about two hours. New legislation governing emissions from crematoria means the cost is rising.

The conveyor belt funeral

There have been concerns about the 'conveyor belt funeral'. The truth is that most crematoria are uninspiring places, and you are allocated a 20-minute slot. In some crematoria it can be as long as 45 minutes and in others as brief as 13 minutes, so there is the feeling of being rushed through to make way for the next coffin (which you are).

Many crematoria try to address these issues and try to accommodate individual needs and beliefs, as well as allow for more personal ceremonies. Some crematoria allow for a double booking at no extra charge. Crematorium staff are usually helpful and supportive and are happy to talk things through with whoever is organising the funeral.

Having your own funeral pyre

All decisions issued by English courts, and incidental comments by judges in relevant court cases, clearly state that cremating a body on private land is not illegal, providing it doesn't cause a 'nuisance' (i.e. unacceptable pollution or smell).

However, some civil servants responsible for giving advice on the matter disagree. Consequently, it is possible that someone might be taken to court to finally prove the matter one way or the other.

There was a high profile case in the Summer of 2006, where a young Sikh man was cremated on a funeral pyre in the north of England. The organiser hopes to have the legality confirmed in the English and European courts.

Legal expert John Bradfield advises that you should consult with a professionally insured lawyer before deciding whether to go ahead with a funeral pyre. Any high street lawyer is sure to be very cautious and likely to advise you not to go ahead. Other funeral pyres have not attracted publicity. They were later reported to public officials but were not used to test the law. Anyone thinking of going ahead, would be well advised to keep away from public roads, footpaths crossing fields, and other places where there are 'rights to roam'.

Natural burial

Natural or woodland burial provides an ecological alternative to cremation or traditional burial and is becoming increasingly popular. Being buried in a woodland, meadow or nature reserve returns our loved ones to nature, while the land retains its natural beauty and wildlife. Burial usually takes place in a biodegradable coffin, or a shroud, and a shrub, tree or flowers are planted instead of a memorial. The exact site of the grave is carefully recorded, and the cost varies from £500 to £1,000 for a plot.

The first woodland burial site was set up in Carlisle in 1995 by Ken West, the Carlisle bereavement officer, who recognised the need for a more environmental approach to burial. There are now over 200 sites and many more in the planning stages.

Natural burial grounds have provided the space and philosophy for families to 'take back' the funeral process, by doing it themselves and personalising the ceremony. Natural burial sites are owned either privately or by local authorities. Only a few have buildings in which to conduct a service, and many families choose to hold the ceremony at the graveside.

This has its pros and cons, as Rupert Callender points out: "The natural burial movement is still in its infancy. Woodland burial is often a misnomer: most of them don't have any trees yet, and most don't have a ceremonial space on site. So when you're huddling around a wind-lashed grave in February, you're not given much to musing on the nature of life and death. You can have yurts and marquees, but in truth a building is good."

Burial on private ground

> *"We buried a man who died at home at dawn on midsummer's morning. His family built his coffin out of wood that he'd grown, and buried him in a wood that he had planted 20 years ago. We put 150 candles on the site and the family spent the day weaving a wild flower bower for everyone to walk through. The whole village was there, and at the end his grandsons set off some fireworks and we toasted him with the last home-made wine he made. But that's one percent, most people can't do that."*
>
> Rupert Callender

There are records of Quakers being buried in their gardens as far back as the 17th century. Burial on your own land is surprisingly easy. John Bradfield of the AB Welfare and Wildlife Trust is the foremost authority on the law relating to funerals. He says: "Planning permission is not required for non-commercial sites, for a limited number of burials for family, friends and those living in the house."

Private burial myths

The following points are wrong and are simply popular myths:

* There must be no house within a 100 yards of a grave.

* The minimum depth for the body or coffin is six feet.

✳ A coffin must be used.

✳ Undertakers and a hearse must be used.

✳ The local council's environmental health department must be informed.

✳ The police must be informed.

✳ If the person died of a notifiable disease they may not be buried at home.

✳ Burials are a health risk and quicklime should be used.

There is no legal requirement to inform any organisation in advance, such as your local environmental health department or the Environment Agency. John Bradfield says that public officials vary from being very helpful and sensitive to authoritarian and obstructive. He advises to keep well away from public officials, because of the unpredictable risks of consulting with them.

Claims are often made about graves devaluing houses prices by up to 50% but there is no hard evidence of any devaluation examples as yet. However, unless the grave area is not sold with the land, the house price may be affected one way or the other – depending upon who is buried there.

Private burial musts

✳ In Eire it is necessary to get permission from the Health department.

✳ In England and Wales, the documentation for a burial on private land is the same as for any kind of burial (See Private Burial in Forms and Formalities).

✳ It is a strict requirement of law, that there must be a land burial register, even if it is only for one or a few graves. That register is then passed to successive owners of the land, along with the property deeds. (See private burial in Forms and Formalities)

✳ If you do not own the land, you must have the owner's permission in advance.

✳ If the owner has a mortgage, get the money lender's prior permission in writing.

✳ The grave should be deep enough to prevent any smell and not be near any well or bore hole. The Environment Agency and your local authority have details about all wells and boreholes. The grave must not be within ten metres of any standing or running water, or 50 metres from a well, borehole or spring that supplies water for human consumption.

✳ Check that burials are not prevented by restrictive covenants on the land. Some covenants can be altered.

✳ It is dangerous to dig deep in very sandy soil.

✳ Avoid land where the grave would start to fill with water.

✳ The burial must not cause a 'nuisance' such as smell or pollution.

✳ Technically speaking, the Environment Agency is entitled to carry out works to prevent pollution of 'any controlled waters'. However, it only expects to be consulted in very rare circumstances, as it has said that there is no evidence of any pollution from any burials.

Recommendations

✳ Choose a garden big enough, so as not to cause offence

✳ There should be two or three metres of soil above the coffin

✳ Keep a plan of where the body is with your deeds. The burial may affect your house price.

Selling the land

It is a good idea, if you will be selling the land, to consider whether land on which the grave is situated could be separated and kept in trust. Try to position the grave so it can be separated from any land which might be sold. Another option is to retain the 'burial rights', along with access rights, otherwise future owners of the land might find a way to have the body exhumed, although this is rare.

Burial at sea

This is a nice idea, but very complicated. In short, the Department for Environment, Food and Rural Affairs (Defra), understandably, does not want bodies being washed up on our coasts or caught in our fishing nets. There are only three places in the UK where sea burial is allowed: Newhaven, west of the Isle of Wight, and near the mouth of the Tyne.

Burying a body at sea means you will have to weigh the coffin and the body down with a huge amount of metal, about 1,000kg, find a willing funeral director and, if you haven't got access to one, charter a private yacht. Contact Defra for more information [*Helpline: 08459 335577 www.defra.gov.uk*].

Green funerals

"*A green funeral is the natural burial of an unembalmed body in a biodegradable coffin, in a natural burial ground, where the* memorial is a living thing – a tree or a plant. But any funeral can be made greener."

Mike Jarvis, Director, Natural Death Centre

Ways to be greener include:

✳ a biodegradable coffin

✳ no embalming

✳ natural burial ground

✳ no flowers with Oasis, cellophane or wire

✳ wild flowers

A cremation or traditional burial can be made greener with a little thought and planning. And the good news is that green burials are cheaper than traditional burials. As Rupert Callender says: "The green funeral movement is a social movement as well as an environmental one; it's about getting family involved in each stage of the process. People usually come to us from an environmental angle, because their mother died and made certain requests – perhaps she said she wanted a cardboard coffin. Then they realise they can have whatever type of funeral they choose. That can be very liberating."

Our churchyards are full and our cemeteries are filling up. Land on this tiny island is ever an issue and there simply isn't enough to give everyone their allocated six feet under. Our cemeteries, with their well tended lawns, use fertilisers and weedkiller.

The truth is we bury our bodies too deep in the earth to actually feed the soil and we are instead eventually washed away in the ground water, so it is something of a myth that we contribute to pushing up the daisies.

Unfortunately, cremation is an ecological nightmare: 400,000 bodies are cremated each year, consuming £3 million of gas in the process and spewing poisonous mercury from amalgam dental fillings into the air, as well other noxious chemicals released from veneer coffins and embalming fluids.

Nearly 1.4 tonnes of highly toxic mercury entered the atmosphere thanks to crematoria in 2000 alone, according to DEFRA. So bad is the problem that the Department has recently ordered crematoria to halve their mercury emissions by 2012, at an estimated cost of £168 million – a cost that will ultimately be passed on to the bereaved. Much is being done to reduce these emissions and find ecological alternatives, but there is no easy solution.

Woodland burials provide a good alternative. We need more trees and we need to address the challenges with regard to agricultural land and social land and how the two intermix. We also need stronger environmental protection for our countryside.

In dense urban areas cemeteries are being re-used. The remains are buried deeper into the earth to make way for new ones, in a process called 'lift and deepen'.

The future

Several new alternatives are in the early stage of development to provide a greener alternative to the traditional choices of burial or cremation.

Promession

Susanne Wiigh-Mäsak, a Swedish biologist, has pioneered a process called Promession. It is an eco-alternative to cremation or burial, and in her native Sweden she has won over bishops, rabbis, funeral directors and the government.

The process involves taking the body in a simple coffin and freeze drying it in liquid nitrogen. The 70 per cent water content of the body evaporates, and the body is mechanically vibrated at a specific frequency to transform it – and the coffin – into organic dust. The dust, weighing in at between 20-30kg, is buried in a shallow grave in an eco-friendly coffin that rapidly decomposes into compost. A tree, shrubs or flowers can be planted directly on the grave.

Mercury and other toxins are removed after freeze-drying, and as no embalming fluid is used the whole process is much less ecologically damaging. Susanne has tested the method with pig carcasses and planted roses above the containers with what she says are "excellent results". A passionate gardener, her love of the soil gave her the inspiration for Promession: "I see myself as well organised compost on my way to biodegradation. I am, therefore I mulch." She extols the virtues of composting at every opportunity.

Her goal is simple: "Respect. Most of all, respect for the living soil and the possibility to keep on living on this planet." She describes herself as: "a consommé; a concentration of all the food I have eaten in my lifetime. I gave my body everything from the soil and I owe my body back to the soil. It's economy – everything you take out you must put back. Now we are six billion on this planet, all taking something from the soil, and when we return to the soil we are washed into the ocean. Or by burning, we are in the air. Nobody is giving anything back. Promession is about putting us back into the cycle. It is about how we can reconnect with the Earth."

Resomation

Resomation is a process originally pioneered for use in medical schools in the US. It is an accelerated version of the natural decomposition process, using an alkali/water mix at very high temperature. The remains are nourishing to the land and come in two forms, bio-ash or bone 'shadows', very similar to cremated remains, and a liquid containing the amino acids, salts, sugars and minerals that make us who we are. The idea is that we are returned to our constituent elements.

The body is placed in a 'resomator' in a silk coffin, and the process takes about two hours. It would cost about the same as cremation, and although at the time of writing it is not a legal alternative to cremation or burial, the Glasgow-based company has received much interest from crematoria, and hopes to begin installing resomators in crematoria imminently.

Choosing a coffin

For hundreds of years we used to bury our people in a woollen shroud: it was the government's way of subsidising the wool industry. Coffins came with the Victorians, and the more elaborate the better. They were fashioned from fine wood and furnished with metal. In the 1950s the coffin changed from being the realm of the local carpenter to the province of the funeral director. Wooden coffins were replaced with a cheaper chipboard alternative, veneered to look like wood.

An American casket maker I met told me that his fellow countrymen for the most part prefer to be buried in traditional wooden caskets, and metal caskets are still resoundingly popular. Whereas once we needed to protect ourselves from the encroachment of the earth, or make a more elaborate exit into the fire, these days we seem more prepared to strip these layers away, and our coffins reflect that.

Chipboard coffins are not very eco-friendly as they contain formaldehyde, which is poisonous to the earth and the air. Coffins are now available in a vast array of materials from cardboard to bamboo and willow, water hyacinths or banana leaves. There is no legal requirement for a coffin, but the dignity of the dead and the sensibilities of the living demand there is some covering.

Bury me in water hyacinths

Here's a round-up of the different coffins you can choose from. [*You'll find a list of contact details on our website —see the back of this book for more details.*]

Cardboard coffins – forget the cereal box connotations; cardboard coffins are really strong and can look great. They come in different colours, with marble or wood effects, and can be decorated.

Eco-pods – a fantastic design based on an ancient Egyptian design and made of recycled paper. They are available in different colours.

Bamboo and willow coffins – eco-friendly and beautifully made by hand. Many people decorate these coffins with flowers, threading them through the weave.

Untreated pine coffins – these come flat-packed but are easily assembled.

Wooden coffins – The more traditional coffins comes in solid oak, pine or beech, or you can get untreated versions, or veneered chipboard.

Make your own coffin – the *Natural Death Handbook* contains plans to make a simple coffin, or you could commission your local carpenter to make one.

Coffins for children – most of these coffins come in small sizes for children. Heaven on Earth in Bristol supply beautiful wooden coffins for the very young.

Coffins as art – artists can be commissioned to paint a simple wooden or cardboard coffin, or you can do it yourself, or enlist friends and family.

Papier maché – Andrew Vaccari makes beautiful papier maché coffins.

Coffins as furniture – the idea of having a piece of furniture that is later used as a coffin was pioneered by the brilliant Heaven on Earth, Bristol's innovative life and death shop. They make bookcases and trunks that can be well used and well loved and with you until the very end.

Crazy Coffins – Vic Fearn near Nottingham are traditional casket makers who have branched into themed coffins. This is not a new idea – traditionally Ghanaian coffins are shaped to reflect the life and loves of the person – so a coffin could be shaped as a car, a shoe or even a beer bottle. Vic Fearn coffins are beautifully designed and made and the company has been commissioned to make coffins as skateboards and guitars. When I spoke to them they were making an exact replica of a Pullman carriage.

Heaven on Earth similarly make made-to-order coffins including replicas of the Red Arrow aeroplanes. They also make and supply more simple coffins.

The cost of a coffin

A coffin can cost any thing from under £100 for a cardboard coffin, to several thousand. The handmade artist-designed coffins are going to reflect the workmanship required. Wicker, bamboo and other natural coffins range from £300 to £600.

Wicker does vary in quality; Somerset Willow makes the crème de la crème.

Buying a coffin

Most coffins listed here are available straight from the manufacturer and can be delivered within two days. More traditional coffins are also available from a supplier, but shop around as prices vary wildly. It's really nice to be able to see the coffin before you buy it. Some funeral directors will stock them.

Make sure you know the height, weight and shoulder width of the person. Also check if the handles are weight-bearing or just ornamental.

Natural burial grounds ask that biodegradable coffins are used, and in some cases can supply them.

For cremation, biodegradable coffins are more common now. Some crematoria and cemeteries sell cardboard coffins. If coffins are painted, water-based paints must be used. Crematoria ask people not to use sawdust or plastic as lining.

Coffin linings

Traditionally coffins were lined with sawdust but cloth, cotton, old blankets or pillows can be used. Many companies offer a lining of soft cotton, silk or other natural materials. For cardboard coffins a body bag is often used. You may approach your local funeral director, but there are some direct suppliers, and biodegradable types are available.

Coffin covers

A drape in beautiful cloth is sometimes used over the coffin. This could hide the cardboard nature of a coffin.

Re-usable coffins

These are a pioneering idea from Ken West, who was Carlisle Council's bereavement manager, to use a beautiful wooden coffin at the crematorium, with a cardboard one inside which would be removed before entering the cremator.

Shrouds

Shrouds are an alternative to a coffin and can be made from wool or silk. Green Fuse in Totnes have a kit to make your own. Green Fuse also sell a beautiful felt shroud made by Yuli Somme, which was displayed in their window in Totnes, Devon. People I spoke to thought it was lovely and liked the idea of being wrapped up in a soft blanket.

The remarkably pioneering people at Carlisle cemetery office have designed their own shroud, which comes complete with board and ropes.

Urns

As well as the vast array of traditional urns there are beehives or mud huts, or an urn version of the eco-pod, or bamboo urns. You can commission an urn from a potter. The Neptune sea urn is made from compressed sand and salt, looks beautiful and slowly dissolves in water.

Gil's funeral – Valerie's story

When my husband, a devout Catholic, died I decided that as an atheist I could not have him buried by a priest uttering sentiments with which I had no sympathy – I would have felt like a charlatan.

My husband, who was 86, had fallen down the stairs. The doctor told me that he had a hemorrhage to the brain and there was nothing that could be done.

Early on Saturday the whole family, including grandchildren as young as six, gathered round my husband's bed and, as if he had waited for that, he gave up his fight and quietly slipped away. I know it is fashionable nowadays to shield children from death, but I feel it is important that they experience it as part of life.

I went out to my car, intending to have a quiet weep on my own, but once again pragmatism came to my rescue. I would have a houseful for the weekend and they would all have to be fed. So, five minutes after my husband died, I stood in the butcher's ordering, through my tears, ribs of beef, sausages and chicken.

Over lunch, we discussed the practicalities of what to do next – death certificate, undertakers, and burial.

After much thought, I decided a simple interment in the ground, with close friends and family by my side, would be the ideal arrangement. I wanted nothing 'commercial', no elaborate wreaths that benefited only the florists, no extravagant coffins. It would be as natural and organic as possible. I knew this would not go down well with my Catholic acquaintances, who would be appalled at the thought of a godless ceremony when my husband had been such an ardent believer, but he had several times voiced total disinterest in what happened to his body once he had died. Luckily, the children felt the same as I did and were only too anxious to help.

My daughter lives in rural Devon, not far from my son, and she was able to obtain permission for her father to be buried in a beautiful sloping field overlooking the green undulating countryside – a field that had only recently been opened as a burial ground. Since it belonged to the village and not the church, anyone with a connection to the village could be interred there. The first hurdle of 'where' had been overcome; now it was 'how'.

One of my son's friends had set up a 'green' funeral service and we enlisted his help in obtaining a coffin made of interwoven reeds, into which my son and daughter laid my husband after they had dressed him. It is common practice nowadays to leave such things to the professional undertaker, but my children wanted to perform this last office for their father.

But first we had to collect the body from the coroner's office where there had been an autopsy. We obtained a certificate for burial (the death certificate would not be available for some days), and debated how to get the body to Devon. On measuring, my daughter's car proved to be too short, and understandably she didn't fancy careering around the country with a cadaver in the back – imagine explaining that to the police if someone in the Little Chef car park became suspicious! My son's friend came to the rescue with his large Volvo estate and he and my son drove up to London, collected the body and took it back to Devon.

On the day of the funeral, we drove to the village square: five friends, two children, four grandchildren and me. We walked down a country path to the field where a lone piper played (I have always loved the bagpipes and my mother-in-law was from Orkney). The coffin was already at the burial site; the rush basket interwoven with ivy and a few simple flowers was so unlike the conventional coffin that one friend said that he thought we had come to bury him, not float him down the Nile. Everyone laughed and the air of gloom immediately lightened.

Then, one by one, we each related some anecdote about him and, as several were humorous, the tears were punctuated with laughter. My nine year old grandson had composed a somewhat ghoulish poem in honour of the occasion and this was greeted with both merriment and praise. We adults tend to use euphemisms on such sad occasions but children have no such inhibitions. After the men present had lowered his body into the ground, we each of us threw a flower on to the coffin and a few spadefuls of earth were added.

As we walked back across the field and up the steep lane, the mournful yet encouraging sound of the piper playing *Flowers of the Forest* followed us, slowly fading as we drew further away.

A table had been booked in a private room at the village pub and we repaired there for drinks and lunch. We all agreed that it was the best funeral we had ever been to – no sermons, no gloomy silences and stifled sobs and, above all, no second-hand potted biography from a priest unacquainted with the deceased. In the company of family and intimate friends, we had been able to behave naturally without having to play to the crowd.

Some weeks later, we held a party at home for all my husband's friends and acquaintances to celebrate his life; by then our emotions were not so volatile and we were able to put on a public face.

I hope my children will do the same for me when I die but since I won't be around to care, they must do as they see fit. ∗

CHAPTER 4

Planning the ceremony

"Some say this is supposed to be a celebration of Mary's life," the priest said, "and we'll get to that, but not right now. Right now it hurts too much. We must first mourn her death."

Thomas Lynch – Booking Passage

"Everybody's life deserves an explanation, everybody's life means something. Even if the lesson isn't for them, it's for us, it's for society, it's for their friends, and that is what a funeral is about. It's a huge opportunity for personal growth, and that trickles down from the people who are most severely affected. But everyone involved has a huge opportunity and someone needs to stand up and talk honestly about them, and I'm not talking about being nasty, or vindictive, but it has to be about honesty. When you are truthful it works."

Rupert Callender

The funeral ceremony is about how we choose to say goodbye to the one we have lost and loved. It is a chance to articulate feelings, express grief and celebrate the life and essence of that person. How we do it is our decision. There are no rules, no absolutes here. A ceremony can be religious or secular, conducted by a minister, the funeral director, or family, it can be formal or very informal. These are the moments when we consign the person we have lost to the ground or to the flame, this is where our relationship with the actuality of the person ends and they go to somewhere else, the next life, to heaven, to eternity, to nothing. Whatever our beliefs it is about acknowledging that they are no longer here.

A funeral ceremony is both a mourning of a death and a celebration of a life. It should allow us to consider our own lives and place within the world. It is to provide comfort for the bereaved and reinforce the strength of the family and community left behind.

> *"I remember my father travelling an hour to a funeral, and coming back in high indignation saying, 'I went all that way and the minister's speech lasted 90 seconds – 90 seconds! That man lived for 90 years.'"*
>
> Rev Peter Jupp – the Cremation Society

Simon Smith of Green Fuse says, "If you ask a funeral director for ideas for a ceremony they'll send you a list of hymns. They won't tell you that you can do things that are really different. Or if you say you're not religious you get a humanist, but there's nothing between the humanist and the vicar."

Choosing the time and place

Our rites and our rituals are defined by us, and so define us and our relationship to death. The Quakers bury their own in silence and with absolute simplicity, the Maori people wail in a great release of emotion. Chinese custom is a series of rituals that last for days before the funeral. One African people take the bones of their dead out every year. We memorialise, eulogise, we despair in our own ways.

When the Great Wars came and it was no longer appropriate to hold elaborate funerals and grieving rituals, our funerals became simpler, our grief more private, and our ceremonies more about the formality than the loss, the tradition more than the individual.

> "All races and all religions for all time have been compelled to have a ceremony to mark these rites of passage. It's about honouring this life of ours and valuing our shared humanity, our

> universal human journey. We stand together and bear witness to
> the joy and pain of life's transitions. The unborn to the born, the
> unmarried to the married, the living to the dead."
>
> Sue Gill

Church ceremonies

In these days of fragmented spirituality a ceremony in a church
may feel inappropriate or hypocritical if the person who died,
and their closest family, were not regular churchgoers.
However, if the purpose of a funeral is to tend to our spirits,
our churches can be beautiful places that transport us from the
humdrum of the everyday into the sacred. Sometimes our grief
needs gravitas, needs to be housed in ancient stone and glass.

The fear of an irrelevant service, conducted by a priest who
does not know the person who died, the reading of scriptures
that mean nothing to the family, punctuated by a droning
organ playing obscure hymns, does not have to be the reality.

Secular ceremonies

Our rites of passage are no longer confined to our churches or
places of worship. Non-religious funeral ceremonies, conducted by humanist officiants, or celebrants, are becomingly
increasingly popular. There were 7,000 humanist funerals in the

UK in 2006. Humanists see the world as rational, based on experience and shared values, and their belief is that this life is the only one we get. In humanist funerals the focus is on the life of the person who died, capturing the essence of their personality.

A funeral officiant will work with you to learn about the person who died and create a fitting ceremony. The Humanist Society has a book called *Funerals Without God*, by Jayne Wynne Wilson that contains some useful advice and ideas for secular ceremonies. However, don't think that dreadful and inappropriate ceremonies are the exclusive province of the church.

The space between

As Rupert Callender points out, many of us don't want a funeral at either of these two extremes. "If you're a Christian there's an awful lot of comfort to be had in the funeral ritual; it works if you believe it. On the other side, if you don't believe it, you're left with the humanists, who are great but they're the other extreme. And most people feel that although they don't go to church, they're part of something bigger, especially after they've lost someone. That's the space we're in, that's the space that 90% of the population is in."

According to the Rev'd Fr Frederick Denman, "There is a gap

between religion and spirituality. Mainstream religion is about 4,000 years old, but spirituality is about 90,000. The Church must not be afraid of looking at other people's traditions. Whatever they are, pagan or Buddhist, everyone has something to contribute."

Who should conduct the ceremony?

The ceremony can be conducted by a minister, a celebrant or officiant, a funeral director or the family. Family-led funerals are becoming more popular, especially at natural burial grounds. Arranging your own ceremony can be an incredibly rewarding experience but can also be an overwhelming process, so it is important to have support and a clear vision.

No ceremony

There does not have to be a service at all, there is a power and reverence in silence. The circumstances around the death may mean emotions are too raw immediately after the death and a memorial ceremony held later is sometimes more appropriate.

Where and when

The ceremony usually takes place with the coffin present and does not have to be at the burial site or crematorium.

No licence is needed for a funeral ceremony. It could be at home, in the garden, in a natural burial ground, or at your local pub or village hall, as long as there are adequate facilities, space and a degree of privacy.

Traditionally funerals were held on a week day, but weekend funerals are becoming more popular, especially for natural burial, as they allow for more time and people are freer. However, funeral directors, crematorium or cemetery staff may charge extra for weekend funerals.

The ceremony

"A ceremony is to help the bereaved to accept the fact that the person has died. If it is a sudden death, the funeral should take it out of the abstract."

Claire Callender

"People want to be touched, and I think the funeral is such a good opportunity to do that. People should leave feeling uplifted."

Rev'd Fr Frederick Denman

"What we are trying to do is take away anything that is irrelevant, anything that stands in between you and the experience. If

you take all that away you don't have to replace it with 'and now we're going to release rainbow-coloured doves'– you just take it away, and that space naturally fills up with something, which is mainly that person being honest and truthful. That's all you need to do. That space will be filled with love."

Rupert Callender

The order of service

"I had printed an order of service and another sheet with four photos of her at different stages of her life so people could see her. There was a picture of her when she was 18 and she was so beautiful. I think people really appreciated having that."

from Jan's story [see Chapter 7]

If you choose to have an order of service, it can be printed for people to take with them as a memento, or as a keepsake for those who could not come. Alternatively you can write your own and get it photocopied. Many have a photograph of the person who died, but it's really up to you.

This is a typical structure for a ceremony:

* Music to enter
* Welcome
* Words on life and death

∗ Tributes, the eulogy

∗ The committal

∗ Closing words

∗ Music to leave

Make it personal

The crucial thing is to make the ceremony a true and personal reflection of the person who has died. The Rev'd Fr Frederick Denman explains, "From the beginning, I customise the funeral, I go and see the people, talk to them, look at photographs, I find out who the family are, if they are married. Whether it was a happy marriage is very important. You don't want to say 'sadly missed' when the opposite may be true.

"I sometimes call it a parting ceremony − a parting of friends − and we thank God for who they were, their attributes, their honour, their poise, their hatred of humbug.

"A funeral is a family affair so the more involved they are the better. I always ask the family to say something but the English reserve, because they're in church, means they often don't want to. But a few words can make a huge difference. I held one funeral for an old man. He had no family and only four people came including his solicitor and a chap he knew in the Navy. I asked them, 'Please, say something,' so they all told stories about him. Even to this day they still remember the funeral fondly."

The eulogy

The eulogy is at the centre of the ceremony and should acknowledge the grief in the loss, and celebrate the life that was led, and finally help those present to begin to let go. Traditionally, the eulogy is written and read by the person you have chosen to conduct the ceremony. However, it can be written by a member of the family or a friend and read by them or, as this is a highly charged moment, by someone else on their behalf.

A eulogy doesn't need to sentimentalise or idealise a person. It can contain their history, their achievements, the challenges they faced, their individual quirks or traits, the things that made them who they were. A eulogy can talk about their beliefs, their spirit and those they left behind. It should offer solace in loss and celebrate the beauty of each of us.

You don't have to be the poet laureate to write a eulogy, but if you want his advice, see *Well Chosen Words – how to write a eulogy*, with a foreword by Andrew Motion, free from Co-op Funeralcare

How to find the right words

> *"Music and poetry, that's what they're there for."*
>
> Rupert Callender

For all time it has been the poet's role to capture the essence of experience, when we cannot find words. At times of great joy and immeasurable sadness we turn to the poets. It may be that the person who died had a favourite poem or writer; otherwise there are some wonderful anthologies for funerals that capture many emotions. Does it get more heart-breaking than the *Four Weddings and a Funeral* reading of Auden's poem?

Some favourite poems for funerals

Do Not Go Gentle Into That Good Night	*Dylan Thomas*
All Is Well	*Henry Scott Holland*
Do Not Stand At My Grave and Weep	*Mary Frye*
A Navaho Prayer	
He Wishes for the Cloths of Heaven	*WB Yeats*
Nothing Gold Can Stay	*Robert Frost*
Any poem by Mary Oliver	

There are some wonderful anthologies of beautiful, rich and poignant poems [see *www.whiteladderpress.com for more information*].

Music

"The trouble with hymns is that they can be doctrinal, full of dogma, 'purging stains' and so forth," says the Rev'd Fr Frederick Denman. "But there are some powerful songs from musical theatre. *When You Walk Through a Storm* – for some people that means everything. But it has to be done well. I've had people who say 'I want this for Mum,' and they bring in a little ghetto blaster to an enormous church and it sounds pathetic. There must be a good sound system, or live music. I never tell people what to play. For that family anything is suitable."

"Music is huge, so evocative, rarely does someone die and no one knows what music to play. Someone, somewhere knows," says Claire Callender. "We were at Bodmin crematorium recently; a young man had died and his three brothers played *Brothers in Arms* by Dire Straits and held each other and it was like you had never heard the song before."

Her partner Rupert adds, "You don't have to be clever, and think 'Oh, it has to be Eno'. Really cheesy songs can be overwhelming. There is something powerful about communally raising your voice, but if the family can't sing, or the song is really complicated, it can be awful. Take *Abide With Me* – I can't hear it enough times."

The nation's favourite funeral songs

Goodbye My Lover	*James Blunt*
Angels	*Robbie Williams*
I've Had the Time of My Life	*Jennifer Warnes and Bill Medley*
Wind Beneath My Wings	*Bette Midler*
Pie Jesu	*from the Requiem Mass*
Candle in the Wind	*Elton John*
With or Without You	*U2*
Tears in Heaven	*Eric Clapton*
Every Breath You Take	*Police*
Unchained Melody	*Righteous Brothers*

Less conventional requests have been *Going Underground* and *Take My Breath Away*.

The nation's favourite hymns

The Lord is My Shepherd

Abide With Me

All Things Bright and Beautiful

The Old Rugged Cross

Amazing Grace

The Day Thou Gavest, Lord, is Ended

How Great Thou Art

Jerusalem

Morning Has Broken

Love Divine, All Loves Excelling

(Source: Co-operative Funeralcare 2006)

Live music

Whether it is a single voice singing an aria in a cathedral or a New Orleans Jazz band in a field, live music is a wonderful addition to a ceremony. A lone musician at committal can be incredibly poignant. After all, we die as we are born, alone (is that a Madonna song?).

Musicians can be found through the local music school, music shops, or using the joys of the internet. We managed to find a kilted bagpipe player in the heart of Devon. Your minister will talk to you about using the church choir or organist. In general the music played on arrival is usually quieter or more reflective, but music played as people are going out could really be anything.

Space to speak

> *"Then, one by one, we each related some anecdote about him and, as several were humorous, the tears were punctuated with laughter."*
>
> from Valerie's story

It may be that more than one person talks about the person who has died. It may be that during the ceremony or at the committal people are given the opportunity to share their thoughts or memories of a person. Someone's history could be told by several different people.

A flower may be passed around a circle to allow people to speak about the person who died, if they wish to.

> *"A few people stood up and told anecdotes or said a few words – mostly humorous as well as heartfelt. This was a lovely infor-*

mal few minutes which made the ceremony feel as though it was shared between us all, rather than just a 'performance' from the family."

from Roni's story

Honest words

Honesty is the straightest route to finding meaningful words, according to Rupert Callender: "Our best funeral this year was for a man who had died at home. He had battled depression and isolation all his life. We buried him in a woodland burial site and there were five or six of us at the grave. His daughters talked about their father, who had never been the best dad. But these women were magnificent, they just talked honestly about him, it was breathtaking. We released some lanterns at dusk, and the sun came out for the first time all day."

The Rev'd Fr Frederick Denman cautions, "If there is anger that this has happened, there's no use pretending, so I find a prayer or words to express that: 'Lord this isn't good enough'. If the person has had a rough time, there's a lovely prayer from pagan tradition: 'Boatman, ferryman, he's had a rough crossing, Carry him gently in your warm arms of night.'"

Rupert gives another example of honesty creating a beautiful ceremony: "We buried a woman from a very traditional moorland family, on her own land. The family weren't given to great displays of emotion. We carried the coffin out across the fields and the family had tied wildflowers on the tree trunks. We stood around the grave and talked honestly about her and we talked about love, in the simplest way. Everyone was in floods of tears. Afterwards, one of the family members, a farmer, told me he was really nervous about what was going to happen because he didn't know the form, unlike in the crematorium, where everyone knows what's coming. He was worried we were going to make them chant or something, but he was really moved by the experience because it happened naturally."

Words of regret

Sadly, many of us feel regretful about things when someone dies. The Rev'd Fr Frederick Denman advises, "Death is the great moment of truth. If the death is sudden, you are in shock and you may feel 'Oh, I wish I hadn't said that.' There may be regrets, but this is the time when you can put it right. We may sit in silence or listen to a song and I will invite people to speak in the old familiar way of all that fills their hearts to the person who has died. People need to be able to do that. Sometimes they say to me that they really did feel that person's presence and were able to say 'I'm so sorry.' Sometimes people write a note and put it in the grave."

Words of farewell

The Rev'd Fr Frederick Denman says, "At the end we do the farewell and we are thinking about our own mortality, our own vulnerability. Whatever our beliefs we hope we should see them again, and if we leave this place with sorrow in our hearts perhaps we can believe we will some day be reunited."

Words of love

The Rev'd Fr Frederick Denman again: "With the music and what people have said about them, there is the idea that their spirit is with us. I light a candle to symbolise that person burning in our hearts, and how they'll always burn in our hearts. Death is just a new way of loving. I ask them to be sensitive that they loved you in life, they helped you and guided you, so be sensitive that they will continue, and be sensitive that that will happen, and now and again you'll sense their presence."

The committal

"We always get the family to do the bearing, and more importantly lower the coffin into the grave. There's no escaping the finality of lowering your mum, in her coffin, into her grave."

Rupert Callender

This is the actual letting go of the physical form of the person you loved. Whether you are lowering them into the ground or releasing them into the flame, this is when you say goodbye. This is the dust to dust, ashes to ashes moment. For burial it is traditional to throw in a handful of earth, or fill in the grave, or throw petals or flowers onto the coffin.

This is the time to release the rainbow-coloured doves if you wish. Or white doves, or a pigeon, or fireworks, or balloons. Symbolically the spirit is free. Sometimes you won't need to. Sometimes rainbows appear anyway.

"It had been raining off and on all morning, but as the funeral started the rain cleared and the sun came out."

from Roni's story

Children at funerals

Claire Callender says, "I never force people to bring their children, but I keep on asking until they agree. We did one funeral of a little girl where the child was laid out and all her friends who were five and six year old children spent time with her. When you're six, something mind-blowing happens every day, this was just something new. They had no cultural baggage.

"If managed properly, kids can deal with and assimilate grief much better than adults. Children have to be involved, all children, otherwise what do they think happens when people die? They just disappear. If they don't go to the funeral, they don't see the summing up of that life, they don't see how loved that person was, how missed they are. They don't get a chance to say 'Wow my dad meant that much.'"

As Rupert Callender points out, "When we built a massive funeral pyre for a man who had young children, we knew that those children would never forget that, because we had built the biggest fire those boys had ever seen in their lives."

> *I know it is fashionable nowadays to shield children from death, but I feel it is important that they experience it as part of life.*
>
> from Valerie's story

Practicalities

Transport

A hearse is traditional, but a Volvo estate is plausible. A horse and cart, or stagecoach, may be possible, even a VW campervan. There are motorbike and sidecar hearses, and vintage lorries. Coffins have been transported on a flatbed truck, and one family I know of took their mum in a home-made coffin on the roof rack of their Vauxhall estate.

Carrying the coffin

Coffins are always heavier than you think, and traditionally carried feet first on the shoulders of the coffin bearers. Coffin bearers in many cultures are the male family members of the deceased. Funeral directors have their own bearers, if required. Strength is key, and bearers should be chosen with that in mind. Obviously drastic height differences should be avoided.

Make sure that the coffin can easily be accommodated in the space you have chosen and that there are no tight corners or steep stairs. The coffin can also be carried using straps, which are needed for lowering the coffin into the ground. Check that the handles are not just for decoration; most eco-coffins can be carried by handles.

Lowering the coffin into the grave

Three pieces of wood will be placed across the grave and the bearers will lower the coffin on to them. Three long straps, made from upholsterer's webbing will be placed around the coffin. When the time comes the bearers will then hold the straps while someone removes the wood. The coffin can then be lowered into the grave.

Transforming a space

In this commercialised world our dreams are stolen and then repackaged and sold back to us, but people are desperately look-ing for meaning in their lives. The idea of life after death isn't enough. So we need to reclaim our rituals and make them rele-vant, by weaving art and beauty into these occasions.

Sue Gill

At the cemetery or crematorium time is often an issue. It's worth talking to people there to ask if they will allow you to decorate the space. If you have chosen a different place, or your home, gather friends and family and do it together.

"For the service in the crematorium, I wanted to have Mum's cof-fin in the middle, with us sitting in a circle around it. However we were told that it was absolutely not possible to have the cof-fin other than in the prescribed place. The chairs were fixed in rows, so we couldn't move them."

from Jan's story

Here are some ideas for creating the right atmosphere:

* A special cloth or banner or something personal belonging to the dead person to lay on top of the coffin.

* Photographs are especially poignant and lovely for people

to look at. You can get them enlarged or photocopied or create a montage.

✳ Lighting, candles or lanterns.

✳ Incense or herbs and oils.

✳ Paper cuts: shapes cut out of paper and placed on windows.

✳ At one child's funeral, some creative people had made butterflies and hearts out of willow and tissue paper and hung them from the ceiling.

✳ Seating can sometimes be arranged in a circle.

✳ Make sure the sound system is up to the job.

> *"We negotiated with the crematorium manager for a double slot at the beginning of the day to gain time to decorate the space and take it all down afterwards. So we hung the crem with simple big banners in blue and red suspended from theatrical lighting stands, and put sunflowers and marigolds in earthenware vases. We framed it all with strings of small white paper cuts cut with fire and bird imagery, and made it more cosy with pools of warm lighting.*
>
> from the story of Bryan Fox's funeral in *The Dead Good Funerals Book* by Sue Gill and John Fox (2004)

Video and photographic memorials

As a film-maker I have been asked to make films, with a collection of still and moving images, and with music, as a tribute to be shown at the funeral. Moving images of a person are incredibly poignant. It's a lovely thing to do if you can. I filmed a funeral of one man who died who had very young children; the film was for the children to watch when they were older. It was the most poignant film I have ever made.

A photographic record of the funeral can be wonderful for family and friends to look at after the event and provides a record for the people who were not there.

The future

The Callenders, at the Green Funeral Company, have clear views on what funeral spaces ought to be like in the future. Claire says, "Crematoria seem to be designed without bereaved people in mind. They are in municipal buildings which look, at best, like a humanities block from a '70s comprehensive. And they're still building them like that.

"I think that the waiting room should be like a country pub, with a chesterfield and a roaring fire. There should be a bar: people are nervous – they may have to speak – and are seeing people they haven't seen for years. Then you should go into this mind-blowing sacred space that you can make your own."

Rupert agrees: "These buildings should be about user friendliness and beauty, they should have a view, you should be able to see for it miles. We need churches without dogma. Instead of saying 'You're here because Christ died for your sins,' we need to say 'You're here because death is a mystery, and it's central to our lives, and it can reflect back and inform every aspect of our lives – and it should.' Death shouldn't be something that is hidden away in the crematorium, just past the processed food factory."

The Rev'd Fr Frederick Denman has similar views. "I think church services should be about participation. The medieval builders of our cathedrals thought about light, colour and space. It was the Victorians who put in the pews and stained glass and took out the light. I would take out the pews and stand in a circle with the candle on the coffin, so we could turn around and look out. So the service is not just all in here; we take it outside with us when we leave."

Rich's funeral – Roni's story

Rich died very suddenly so I was completely unprepared for organising a funeral. A friend looked in the *Yellow Pages* for me and came back with two options: a traditional funeral arranger or the Green Funeral Company based in Totnes. I remember saying to my step-daughter (the other executor), "It looks like we're going to have to choose between the Christians and the hippies." We settled for the hippies, knowing how Rich would have felt, and because the friend who had phoned up said that the chap who ran the Green Funeral Company (Rupert Callender) sounded lovely.

Rich had put in his will that he wanted to be cremated and his ashes scattered by boat on the River Dart. He also stipulated that he wanted no religious content in the service, and had two pieces of music he wanted played: *Suzanne* by Leonard Cohen, and *Something in the Air Tonight* by Phil Collins.

In fact, Rich and I often used to muse about the sort of funeral or burial we'd like. Well, Rich did more than me as I didn't have such strong opinions as him (few people had such strong opinions as Rich on most subjects). He had often said to me that he'd like a Viking funeral with his body put on a longboat and set ablaze before being floated down the river. I'd told him not to be so ridiculous and I wasn't about to do something complicated and illegal so there was no point in putting it in his will. Then he said it would be great to be buried in the garden ... in his sports car with the roof down, in a sitting position with a silk scarf around his neck wired to look as if it was blowing in the wind. I told him what he could do with that idea too. So what he finally put in his will was much tamer than I'd expected.

Rupert Callender came to visit me and my three grown-up stepchildren to discuss the funeral. To start with I think he realised we weren't happy with the idea of a crematorium service. Our local crematorium is dire, and it just seemed so impersonal and such a conveyor belt process. Rupert suggested that we could book a double slot so that we wouldn't be so rushed, but that didn't solve the other inherent problems. As we talked, Rupert very cleverly picked up on the fact that we were prepared to be quite radical, though we weren't saying so directly because we hadn't realised it was an option.

To be honest, without Rupert I think the funeral would

have been ghastly and would probably have made Rich's death even harder for us all to come to terms with. I don't recall Rupert ever actually making a single suggestion, but somehow he managed to lead us to a really wonderful funeral plan. I remember talking about coffins and he mentioned, in passing it seemed, that one of his recent clients had built a coffin for his mother himself rather than buying one in. Instantly my older stepson's eyes popped out on stalks, as I suspect Rupert knew they would, and he volunteered to build his dad a coffin.

As the conversation went on, I mentioned a funeral Rich had once told me about that had hugely impressed him. He'd been passing a church as a group of Hare Krishnas came out carrying a coffin towards a grave. They were chanting, slowly at first, but it became more and more celebratory. Then they began to bounce the coffin slowly as they carried it. Gradually the coffin was sent higher and higher up until they were literally throwing it several feet into the air and catching it repeatedly. Rich told me that the overall impression was one of joy and celebration of the life that had passed, rather than one of mourning.

At this point, Rupert mentioned a group of Sikhs in the

north of England who had held an open cremation only a few weeks previously. There were all sorts of legal wrangles and they were prepared to go to the court of human rights to defend their traditional customs. All of us were hugely excited by this, and we discussed the possibility of actually cremating Rich in our field below the house. However we were concerned about the legal angle, and also being of a western persuasion we weren't at all sure most of our guests would want to see a body burning, and we weren't confident that anyone we knew had the skills or experience to build a fire guaranteed to be hot enough to prevent this. Eventually we decided that tempting as a private cremation would be, it wasn't for us.

However, the idea had got us really fired up (forgive the pun). It had echoes of Rich's Viking burial schemes, and of the celebratory mood of the Hare Krishna funeral he'd talked about. So we decided on a plan B. We would cremate Rich's body privately at a different crematorium (near Bodmin, where there is a beautiful view of the valley from the main room). Then we would put the ashes in a coffin built by my stepson and hold a funeral service in our field where we would burn this coffin.

From my point of view I think that organising the funeral was an incredibly useful displacement activity. As an ex-stage manager I wasn't daunted, and I had a huge amount of help of course, and it allowed me to keep my mind occupied but still focused on Rich. This was a blessing at a time when I really hardly knew what I was doing. I also have three young children with Rich and I remember one day saying to one of the many people around, "I must give the boys breakfast in a minute," to which my friend replied, "Don't worry, they've already had breakfast. And lunch. And supper." It was 6pm.

The children were a huge factor in planning the funeral. We had two critical aims as far as they were concerned. The first was that we wanted to make sure it was an occasion they would never forget. As my youngest was only four, that meant it had to be pretty memorable. Secondly, we wanted them to enjoy it. That's not easy when it's your own father's funeral, but we were determined it must be possible.

One of the most helpful things Rupert said right at the start was, "Don't feel you have to rush." He slowed the process right down for us so we set the funeral for ten days after Rich's death. Two days before the funeral my three children, my three stepchildren and I made the one-hour drive down to Cornwall to see Rich's body. Rupert lived in an ancient mill house set among fields and woods, and used a little whitewashed barn as a 'chapel of rest', for want of a better term. The setting was perfect and just what Rich would have liked, and we all went in to see his body, apart from one of my boys who chose to see the coffin after the lid was on. It was so peaceful, with no sound but the birdsong, that we were all really pleased we had decided to see him. We took it in turns, and between times my boys played in the field and the stream and Rupert helped them find water boatmen and whirligig beetles in the pond. They got so filthy and wet that I remember he put all their trousers through the tumble dryer for me before we left.

My three stepchildren and I went to Bodmin crematorium where we met Rupert and the coffin with Rich's body in it. We went into the main room (no idea if it has a name) and put the coffin down in front of the curtains. No one spoke, but we all hugged each other and had a good cry for a few minutes. Then one by one we went over to the coffin and finally sent it through the curtains. Then we left, still in silence, and went to pick up the boys and go home. It was deeply emotional, of course, but a very peaceful and beautiful send-off. In a sense though we felt it was just a formality, and had even considered not going. It was only Rich's body, after all. Seeing it earlier had made it very clear that he was absent, and in a sense the cremation at Bodmin was just a technicality in order to convert his body into a different form for the funeral proper two days later.

By Friday morning, there was a massive funeral pyre about 12 feet high in the field. A couple of friends with access to loads of old pallets and timber had provided the materials, and a mate with lifting equipment and suitable experience had helped to design and build the thing. Lots of people mucked in with the construction. There was a wide shelf at the front, about five feet up, for the coffin to sit on.

We had an open-sided marquee in case it rained, and a small tent in which we put a book of remembrance. We also asked everyone who was coming to bring something to put on the fire, and there was a basket which slowly filled up with notes, letters, ribbons and flowers.

Shortly before the funeral we prepared the coffin. We put

Rich's ashes (which Rupert had brought back from the crematorium) in his metal tool box because it was the only thing we could find that we reckoned would withstand the heat so we could salvage them later for scattering on the river. We also put in a bottle of his favourite wine, a bunch of flowers collected from all his favourite plants in the garden, notes and pictures from us and the children, a few favourite objects of his, and a roll-up (he'd given up smoking a few years previously and missed it desperately). Then the coffin was carried down to the funeral pyre.

It had been raining off and on all morning, but as the funeral started the rain cleared and the sun came out.

We'd organised a PA system, and the funeral opened with Rupert saying a few words. There were a few chairs beside him for those of us who were directly involved in the service, and everyone else just stood around or sat in the treehouse. We'd asked Rupert to start by saying that any children present (a lot of the boys' friends had turned up) were welcome to play and parents needn't worry if they were noisy. Rupert then gave a wonderful address that described Rich so well we couldn't believe he never actually knew him.

We asked my father to speak next because we knew he'd be really funny. Anyone who knew Rich would tell you that his sense of humour was his most dominant trait, and he'd never have forgiven us for being overly solemn, despite the awful circumstances. Sure enough, my father's speech was both moving and extremely funny. There were a couple more readings and speeches – only one of my stepchildren felt he wanted and was able to speak – a couple of pieces of music my stepchildren and I had chosen, and then I recited *The Hill* by Rupert Brooke. This was one of Rich's favourite poems and, being hopeless at memorising poetry himself, he often asked me to recite it to him. He sometimes used to say, "I want you to say that at my funeral," with no thought, of course, for whether I'd actually be in the mood for reciting poetry. I think I only got through it because I was saying to him, in my head, "Very funny. Well, you're not going to catch me out that easily. You want me to recite it? OK, just you watch me ..."

Next we had an 'open mike' session where Rupert invited any of the guests to say a few words about Rich. A few people stood up and told anecdotes or said a few words – mostly humorous as well as heartfelt. This was a lovely informal few minutes which made the ceremony feel as though it was shared between us all, rather than just a 'performance' from the family.

Finally, we managed to give Rich the final speech, knowing how he always liked to have the last word. He was an author, and his most successful book had been recorded as an audio book. The company who did this were good friends of ours but based a very long way away and couldn't make it to the funeral. So they'd put together a three-minute section of outtakes, which was very funny and moving at times, and had emailed it to me the day before. I'd played it to all six children ('his' and 'ours') and we'd agreed it had to be played at the funeral. No one else had heard it, but it was imperative all the children were ready for it when it was played, as hearing his voice was very emotional.

After this, we took the basket of notes and flowers from the tent and Rich's six children and his two year old granddaughter carried it over to the funeral pyre and placed all the contents on it. I remember there were several sunflowers which looked beautiful decorating the timber pile. We wanted the boys and Rich's granddaughter to be involved but we didn't want to ask them to stand up and speak in front of everyone as that would have been too daunting. I think we did offer the older ones the option actually, but they declined as we'd expected. So this was a good way to keep them involved without putting too much pressure on them.

Next, Rich's three older children each took one of their younger brothers to help them with the grand finale. They backed off about 20 yards from the pyre. My eldest (aged nine) gave the others a signal by sending up a rocket (he'd never been allowed to light a firework before), and the two grown-up brothers then fired flaming arrows at the pyre to set it alight. They then moved in and helped get it going properly using flaming torches. This was to the Phil Collins track Rich had chosen (for the lines, 'There's something in the air tonight ... I've been waiting for this moment all my life.'). When the music ended, we set off a massive firework display, which lasted about three minutes and was the noisiest I'd ever heard (the people we got in to do it had said that for daylight displays you really need noise, as the visuals aren't so dramatic). We really did send Rich out in a blaze of glory.

All the guests had left by about six or seven in the evening. That left about 25 family and very close friends.

By then the fire had burnt down somewhat and we all sat round it late into the night. We went out for takeaways and ate off our laps sitting on deckchairs. I let the boys stay up later than they ever had before, and one of my fondest memories is of them toasting marshmallows, on improbably long bamboo sticks, over their father's ashes. Rich would have been deeply amused by that. ✳

CHAPTER 5

Funerals for different beliefs

I spent some time in Benares when I first went to India ten years ago. Benares, on the banks of the river Ganges, is India's holiest city and to die there is auspicious on a re-incarnation level. Death is everywhere in this city. There is an intensity here, people travel across the continent to die in this holy city. I leave my hotel only in the early morning and late afternoon. Every time I go out I lose my way in the winding streets past sellers of cloth, chai and pots. I find myself at the burning ghats, where the dead are cremated on the banks of the river. It's cheaper to use gas these days than wood. Often I stop to let a family pass, ringing a bell, carrying their lost beloved, wrapped in cloth, bright colours on a simple wooden stretcher, down to the river. Some of them look tiny. Ceremonies are simple, grief is open and it takes place in the melée of city life. The bodies are lowered on to the fire and burnt. It's very real. I feel strange, calm, almost mesmerized by the fire and what it means. I like the continuity here, that the soul is free, that the river is holy, that we take our loved ones to the flames.

Whether your roots are western or eastern, Christian or Islamic or Hindu, if you are designing a funeral yourself rather than following an orthodox traditional ceremony, there is much to be learnt from the way other cultures commemorate their dead.

Buddhist For Buddhists the funeral is a ceremony to wish the soul well in its next incarnation. The body is viewed in an open casket by those present, as a reminder of the impermanence of life. A simple ceremony, with readings from the Sutras, is followed by a cremation or green burial.

Hindu The belief in reincarnation is at the heart of a Hindu ceremony. The family pray around the body, which is washed and dressed in white. There is a procession with the coffin, sometimes past the favourite places of the person who has died. Before cremation the body is decorated with garlands of flowers and sandalwood, and scriptures from the Vedas or Bhagavad Gita are read. After the cremation mourners must wash and change completely before re-entering the house. A mourning period of 13 days then begins.

Jewish The body is placed in a simple wooden coffin or shroud. After a service there is a slow procession to the grave where the rabbi will recite prayers and Kaddish, the prayer for the deceased. The family will then sit in mourning for seven days after the funeral.

Quaker Informal and simple, the mourners often sit in silent contemplation. They may share thoughts and memories of the deceased.

Sikh Because of the belief in the eternal soul, death is God's will and the funeral is focused on praise for the Almighty. The body will be washed and dressed and prayers said to bless the departing soul. The eldest son will then light the funeral pyre with a naked flame.

Muslim The body will be washed and dressed by close relatives. A ceremony will then take place in the home of the deceased led by a family member or imam. Muslims are buried in a simple ceremony with their head turned right towards Mecca.

Greek Orthodox In this tradition the body is placed into a grave for five years. After this time the bones are taken from the ground and laid out in the sun. They are then interred in a special place in the graveyard.

Michael's funeral – Susannah's story

My dad died in hospital of a lung condition. About eight of his close family and friends kept a vigil by his bedside. His good friend was there, who was a vicar, which helped Dad. He had always had a quiet but very strong religion. We were with him when he took his last breath and passed away. We sat with him for a while; it was very surreal and very moving.

I went home to be with my family. In between his death and the funeral, my brother's wife had a baby. It was so sad that Dad missed seeing the baby only by days.

My dad had left when I was young and now had a second family. They lived a long way away and so we weren't very involved in the ceremony, which I found very hard. Before he died Dad had chosen the psalms and hymns that he wanted; they were pretty obscure. The church was beautiful, and Dad's father was a carpenter and had replaced the pews years ago with beautiful lime washed ones, so this was touching.

I had spoken to Dad about having a wicker coffin, and he liked the idea, so we all decided on a purple one. We decorated it with daffodils and irises and it looked beautiful.

Dad was very traditional but he had this wicked, rude and irreverent side to him and the coffin seemed to reflect that.

There were people at the funeral who represented all the different times of his life, which was lovely. I think it is very difficult to be the other family sometimes, because my sister and brother and I weren't invited to put a flower in the coffin, or to speak about him. It was just a lack of communication, but it was very distressing for me. My husband did stand up and talked about Dad in a funny way, but he was the only one who talked about the irreverent side of Dad.

After the church we all went to the crematorium where there was a very brief and very sad ceremony Then we all went to a hotel and had some food and drinks, and I thanked people he'd known for meaning so much to him.

Families are so complicated, and it's so important to communicate honestly. I wish we'd all had a chance to sit down and plan the funeral together. He was my dad too, and I was left with this terrible empty feeling for so long afterwards.

Six months later it was his 60th birthday, and it seemed

right that we should get together again. We decided to scatter his ashes to commemorate the day, so we took a boat to his favourite place and scattered the ashes there. It was lovely and, for the first time, I felt a sense of peace with his death. ✳

CHAPTER 6

Planning a wake

> "Whatever there is to feel, feel it – the riddance, the relief, the fright and freedom, the fear of forgetting, the dull ache, or your own mortality. Go home in pairs. Warm to the flesh that warms you still. Get with someone you can trust with tears, with anger and wonderment and utter silence. Get that part done – the sooner the better. The only way around these things is through them."
>
> Thomas Lynch – The Undertaking

Most of us know the after-funeral gathering as the wake, but traditionally the wake was the time after the death and before the funeral. The wake is still very much part of Irish culture. As a culture we rarely have these inter-generational meetings, so a funeral often means that a lot of people are seeing each other for first time in years.

"After the funeral there is a palpable change in the energy," explains Claire Callender. "Everyone is relieved to be on the other side; everyone wants a stiff drink. This is the place where the more irreverent stories are told."

The setting

If you don't hold the wake at home, it could be in a room in your local pub or community hall. Family and friends can decorate the venue together in their own way. Photos are really great to have on the walls, and the idea of a book for people to sign is lovely. We've all heard the sentiment 'Oh, have a big party when I die.' But maybe your friends and family just won't want to, as Thomas Lynch points out: "The dead can't tell the living what to feel." Any event has its momentum, and a funeral is the same. People gather, they remember in their own way.

Feeding everyone

As Rupert Callender points out, "Everyone needs to eat, and it's worth getting people in, unless someone says they are happy to make the food, keep the tea topped up, and clear away afterwards. Otherwise, if the wake is at the house, the bereaved can be left with loads of clearing up to do."

Asking people to bring a dish to share is a good idea; thus the catering responsibility is shared and the cost minimised. Maybe, like my mother-in-law, cooking is a comfort and could absolutely not be delegated. My family had ham, egg and chips, my grandfather's favourite food, in his local pub after his funeral.

CHAPTER 7

Funerals for different people

Losing a parent

Losing a parent is its own rite of passage. It is the loss of the person responsible for you, even if you are long past the age of dependence. It is a metaphorical handing-on of the baton of life to the next generation, and all the responsibilities that entails. The death of a parent is often our first encounter with death in our inner circle. It is the confirmation of our own mortality.

Our relationships with our parents are deeply complex, guilt is common, and the funeral is about coming to terms with these feelings, acceptance and letting go. Funerals for parents must take in a generational difference and must respect the wishes of the person in a way that articulates the feelings of those who have been left behind.

Losing a child

> *"When we bury the old, we bury the known past, the past we imagine sometimes better than it was, but all the same, the past, a portion of which we inhabited. Memory is the overwhelming theme, the eventual comfort.*
>
> *"But burying infants, we bury the future, unwieldy and unknown, full of promises and possibilities, outcomes punctuated by our rosy hopes. The grief has no borders, no limits, no known ends and the little infant graves that edge the corners and fence-rows of every cemetery are never quite big enough to contain that grief. "*
>
> Thomas Lynch – The Undertaking

Losing a child is a devastating loss, disrupting the natural cycles of life. We were, after all, never meant to bury our children. It is a loss that is profound and far-reaching. Funerals for children and teenagers affect the community deeply, and these funerals will be cathartic and emotional.

The Rev'd Fr Frederick Denman says, "If it's a child, it's about whatever the family wants. If they all want to wear football kits, that's fine. It's good for parents to have some sort of picture, to imagine where the child is gone. The Celtic idea that we're gathered on a seashore with the child is lovely, and there's a great mist, and out of this mist comes this wonderful boat, and the child gets onto the boat, to the most beautiful island where it's always summer and the trees are in fruit and in blossom at the same time, and it's magnificent.

"It's important to know that they are with us. They must be; their spirit must be here. If you live in the hearts of those you love, you never die."

Hopefully there will be a great deal of support at this time and people will help with preparations. With my own children I have found their ability to process the idea of death and confront it incredible. Funerals for children will express the child as they were and will always remain. The friends of the children may want to speak, sing or express grief in their own way.

> *"By dying young a person stays young forever in people's memories. If he burns brightly before he died, his light shines for all time."*
>
> Alexander Solzhenitsyn

Suicide

Death is an escape from the pain of life. There are many feelings that those close to the person who committed suicide will feel: guilt, anger, despair, regret. The Rev'd Fr Frederick

Denman explains, "With suicide, we think of the vulnerability of all of us. We must never condemn. We don't know where we're going, life is difficult. It happens to all of us that we say, 'We can't take this any more.' We just don't go the whole hog."

Rupert Callender adds: "It's important to say that the manner of his dying was not the manner of his living. Honesty is so important. It cannot be the elephant in the room, and you're pretending they've just died. I did a funeral for a man who killed himself in the most violent way, completely out of the blue. There must have been a temptation for his wife to hide with that, with the shame and the horror, and just have a small family funeral, but she threw it open to the community. She stood next to his coffin and talked about the manner of his death. She directed her anger at him, in front of 200 people, and she talked about how we should all look after each other more, and how his death impacted on all our lives. Then she talked about his life, and it was the most mind-blowing display of honesty I've ever seen."

Unexpected death

"No death, however prepared you think you are for it, is expected by the heart," says Rupert Callender. "But a death that comes out of nowhere – a husband on his way to work; a

teenager in a car – wounds in a unique way. A loving relationship can end on a sour note of triviality, the bad luck bum note
of an argument thrown over a departing shoulder on a rainy
Monday morning. If this happens to you, keep the conversation going. Especially while their body is still here, while you
can still be alone with what remains of who they are. Claim
this privacy. Start a dialogue. It will ring in your ears regardless.
This is not the time to let death get in the way of a good conversation."

With an unexpected death, organising the funeral yourself is
probably too much to deal with emotionally. It is a time for
friends and family to gather, to help. When a death is sudden
the family, and sometimes the whole community, is in shock.
Sometimes a death cannot be explained, it can only be accepted. The funeral should be the beginning of this process.

Violet's funeral – Jan's story

My mum died in a retirement home when she was 92. It
was a good death, and not unexpected. Her body was
taken to our local funeral directors, a small family firm
who are very nice people. Although I knew Mum was
dying, she died sooner than I expected so I hadn't chosen
a coffin or decided what clothes she should wear.

The undertaker dressed her in a shroud and put her in an MDF coffin, with an oak finish and gilt plastic handles. It was not at all what I would have chosen and was expensive – over £400. I knew that you're not obliged to take the coffin that the undertaker uses, so I did a bit of rummaging around on the internet to see what I could find. I didn't think Mum would have wanted a cardboard coffin, even though she was gone. It just seemed a step too far.

Although the undertakers weren't stopping me from finding another coffin, they weren't exactly helping me either. Eventually I found a simple, wooden flatpack coffin, but the only ones in stock were over six feet long and they couldn't make another one in time. Mum was so tiny and it didn't feel right to put her in this huge coffin.

I think the process of saying goodbye is very important, so I went down most days and sat with her. By then Mum was dressed in her own clothes, which was much better than the nylon shroud. The chapel of rest was very small, very Victorian, with plastic flowers and drapes, a very gloomy place. And I kept looking at this coffin. It was perfectly conventional, but didn't look like it had anything to do with Mum. She liked everything plain and hated gilt, so I had an idea. I could remove the handles, but because it would leave holes, I thought how Mum loved to do patchwork, and that we still had some squares left over, so I decided I would decorate the coffin with her patchwork.

At first the undertakers were very reluctant to take the handles off, but they had told me that they were just for decoration, so I knew that it could be done. In the end I had to be very firm with them and insist that I wanted to do this and they agreed. Then they seemed to get into the swing of things, and I stuck the patchwork on the coffin and it looked lovely.

My son had the idea that we should take mum to the crematorium in a VW van. None of us like hearses, and Mum and Dad had owned a camper van for years that they had travelled all over the continent in. Mum absolutely adored her van. A friend kindly offered to lend us theirs, which meant it would save us £250 on a bill which was going to be nearly £2,000, for a very basic cremation.

Then our undertaker told us that the crematorium wouldn't accept the coffin if it arrived in the camper van; they had said it wasn't dignified enough. I was very upset, and spoke to the manager myself. I explained the situation and she agreed to let us bring Mum in the VW van.

For the service in the crematorium I wanted to have Mum's coffin in the middle, with us sitting in a circle around it. However we were told that it was absolutely not possible to have the coffin other than in the pre-scribed place. The chairs were fixed in rows, so we could-n't move them. We were also told that we couldn't control the sound system ourselves.

By this time they were obviously jumpy about us, and were very worried about how long we were going to take. Our undertaker had told us "You've got 20 minutes' action time" and we rehearsed the service to make sure, but when we got there they told us we only had 15 min-utes. However it was too late to change it so we just went ahead.

Despite all of this, it all went very nicely. We decorated the coffin with patchwork, and some beautiful flowers, and draped her favourite rug over it.

I asked people to donate to the Lifeboat Institution instead of buying flowers, but I'd bought some local flowers and put them in a tub by the entrance to the chapel. Mum was carried in from the camper van and about 30 of us all followed into the chapel, where we all took a flower and placed it on the coffin, so everyone had a chance to be with her and say their own goodbye.

My ex-husband had composed some beautiful music and I gave an introduction, then my son and daughter took it in turns to tell Mum's life story. We left a space of about five minutes for people to think about her quietly or say something if they wanted to, which was lovely.

We sang a hymn, although I'm not religious and nor was Mum really, but my children wanted everyone to stand up and sing together. So we sang *All Things Bright and Beautiful* which I know Mum liked and, because she had been a fantastic dancer, we went out to the *Gay Gordons*.

I had printed an order of service and another sheet with four photos of her at different stages of her life so people could see her. There was a picture of her when she was 18 and she was so beautiful, I think people really appreciated having that.

After we left the crematorium, we all went home and had tea at my daughter's house and talked and told stories.

I've been to funerals that seemed to have nothing to do with the person who had died, there was a coffin and a service but it didn't tell you anything about them. But everyone told me how much the day had captured Mum and who she was, and I'm really pleased we were able to do that. ✳

CHAPTER 8

Things to do after you die

This chapter is about how we remember and honour our dead. I really hadn't wanted to go into the fanastical 'Hey, you could be a reef,' but I found myself unable to help it. I was particularly excited about having my ashes pressed into a vinyl record, so I could 'live on from beyond the groove.'

Memorials

What is a memorial? Is it our raging against mortality? Is it a place to go, to sit quietly among memories? Is it a chance to do one last thing? Memorials are as diverse as memories. How would we want those we loved to remember us? Standing by a cold stone statue of the Buddha, by a robin splashing in a little stone bath, sitting on the wind-wild cliffs, a tree in woodland ever reaching to the sun? There is no rush to choose a memorial, give yourself time for the dust to settle, the heart to slowly mend, the ground to harden again.

The Rev'd Fr Frederick Denman is clear about what a memorial should be. "Good memorials should name and honour the person, they should say what the person was – maybe he was a boatbuilder – which is important I think. They should be a comfort to the bereaved and something uplifting for people passing by in later years. Some of the words I use in funerals I've got from old memorials: 'You shall climb and reach the top of everlasting hills, where the winds are cool and the sight is glorious'."

A memorial service

A memorial service is a time for gathering weeks or months after the funeral, when emotions have had a little time to settle. This may be a good time to break bread and share stories among a wider circle of friends. There may be a service, some words shared and music played. It could be a ceremony to scatter the ashes. If the person was a public figure or had a wide influence then a memorial is an opportunity for the wider community to pay their respects. The memorial service is a way of affirming life, to remember the dead and celebrate who they were.

In many cultures the passing of a year since the death is marked with a candle lighting, a ceremony, a meal.

The Mexican Day of the Dead

Los Dias de los Muertos is the annual fiesta on which the spirits of the dead are reunited with the living. Taking place from All Hallows Day, 31st October, to All Saints Day, 2nd November, the festival is a time of joyous reunion, remembrance and feasting as families gather together and honour their loved ones who died.

The Natural Death Centre organises a Day of the Dead in April with art, music, celebration and discussion to help us commemorate our dead and think about our own death.

> *"The Mexican is familiar with death, jokes about it, caresses it, sleeps with it; it is one of his toys and his steadfast love."*
>
> Octavio Paz
> Mexican poet, writer and diplomat

Headstones

I was in Brittany this summer, on the wild windblown coast, where 5,000 years ago man buried his dead in chambers of stone and carved images. We have long honoured our dead with stone: witness the crumbling, atmospheric, Victorian graveyards with their angels and effigies, their poems, wisdom and witticisms that comfort and remind us of our own mortality.

I love the way nature takes back the stone, and I like to subtract the dates to find the age of the person who died, and wonder. These old cemeteries are part of our heritage and preserved so. Our latter-day cemeteries are less rambling and more regimented. Stone is now imported from all over the world and letters can be computer generated rather than carved.

It is important to get different quotes and look at the work of the person you have chosen. Crematoria and cemeteries have regulations on the size and type of memorial they will accept, so it is important to consult with them before you decide. Natural burial grounds normally do not accept stone memorials and relatives can plant a tree or flowers and sometimes have a wooden plaque.

A place to go ... or not go

"It is important there is a place to go, and be with the spirit. The general is made real in the particular. I feel people need a space. To tend the grave, place a flower, it is important to go there. I invite people to bury the ashes, so they have that."

Rev'd Fr Frederick Denman

"I spoke to a family, and the grave of their mother was a long way away from where they live and it became this burden. They

felt so guilty that they hadn't cut the grass, or been there to tend it, they almost wished it wasn't there."

Claire Callender

Alternative memorials

Today, pressures on our land use and concerns for the environment mean some of us choose to remember our dead in different ways, and there are now many alternatives to the traditional headstone. [*See the back of the book for how to contact the companies mentioned below.*]

Benches, sculptures and stiles, signs, gates or fences The Stile Company can help with it all.

A celebration box Artist Yvonne Malik has designed a celebration box, a kind of miniature art gallery to fill with keepsakes and memories of the person who has died. It can contain special things, poems, trinkets, a favourite hat, souvenirs. It can be placed in the venue for the funeral and kept forever after.

Memorials by artists Memorials for Artists helps people commission artists to make individual memorials. The charity helps with every stage of the process, including getting permissions from graveyards and cemeteries, and is has contacts with many craftspeople. Commissions range from headstones to sundials and urns.

Memorial tree planting If you want to plant a tree in your local park, or some other public place, contact your local authority. There are now several organisations which arrange for a dedicated tree to be planted in a woodland.

Scattering the ashes

"A person's ashes weigh about the same as a newborn baby. There's a great balance in that."

Rupert Callender

"We always tell people to wait, really think about it before you go and throw the ashes off some headland," Rupert Callender advises. "I learnt this when my father died. Years later I wanted to visit him somehow and his ashes were nowhere. If you are going to scatter them it may be worth keeping some back and putting them in a special box and, if there are young children, keeping some for them."

Scattering the ashes at a beloved place is a symbolic way of saying goodbye to a person, a ritual for family and friends. Sometimes the ashes are scattered to mark a particular anniversary.

"Six months later, it was his 60th birthday, and it seemed right that we should get together again. We decided to scatter his

> *ashes to commemorate the day, so we took a boat to his favourite place and scattered the ashes there. It was lovely and, for the first time, I felt a sense of peace with his death."*
>
> from Susannah's story

Practicalities

There is no law governing the scattering of ashes but you should get the permission of the landowner. If scattering ashes on water it is important to make sure you are a good distance from any water to be used for drinking, agriculture or recreational uses.

The ashes or 'cremains' amount to about 2kg and will be given to you by the crematorium or funeral director in a simple container. The ashes can be buried in a garden; it's a good idea to keep them in a casket if there is a possibility of moving house.

Alternatively the ashes can be placed at a cemetery or crematorium. It may be possible to inter the ashes in an existing family grave and inscribe a memorial vase or name plate, if there is no room on the headstone. Crematoria have a Book of Remembrance, which can be viewed on the anniversary date and is the simplest form of memorial. Ashes can be placed in the Garden of Remembrance, usually beautifully tended and dedicated to the dead of all religions. You can then have an individual memorial within the gardens if you choose. Some crematoria have a columbarian or remembrance wall in which to keep the ashes. This is a good idea for retaining cremated remains until the death of a partner, when both cremated remains can be placed together.

Less conventional memorials

Ashes in orbit Psychedelic guru Timothy Leary had his ashes blasted into space. Hunter S Thompson's ashes were blasted in fireworks from a four-storey iron fist. Costs range from £400 to several million and Heaven Above Fireworks can arrange both (maybe not the fist).

Ashes as diamonds. Your ashes can be made into a gem. The process takes 16 weeks and costs about £3,000.

Ashes as art Ashes can be incorporated into glass to make a vase or paper weight, or mixed with clay to make a statue.

Ashes as reefs An American company mixes the cremains into 'reef balls', which are placed off the coastline of Florida.

Ashes as vinyl Andvinyly can press your ashes into a vinyl record, choose a soundtrack, record a message or just hear your pops and crackles, to 'live on from beyond the groove'.

And finally ...

Cryonics This is an eerie process by which the deceased is frozen and preserved with the idea that science will have advanced, so resuscitation might be possible in the future. It is possible in the UK but not very common. Pioneered in the USA, for those who cannot let go. Cost: around £150,000

CHAPTER 9

Forms and formalities

This section deals with the practicalities of a death, how to look after the body yourself, who to inform, how to register a death, arrange a burial, cremation or private burial, and also funeral formalities, notices and protocol.

Laying out a body

Washing

* Washing the body can be a tender and loving experience:

* Use two people

* Antibacterial soap, oils and incontinence pads will be useful

* It is usual to remove jewellery, and necessary for cremation

Keeping the body at home

✳ Choose a room that is cool, open the windows, close the curtains and turn off the heating

✳ Ice cubes wrapped in cloth can be kept near the body

✳ If the body is to be kept more than 48 hours, or in summer, hire an air conditioning unit

✳ Use deodorising air gels, essential oils, or herbs and flowers to reduce odour. Sealing the coffin lid will also help with this.

✳ Advice kindly provided from *The Natural Death Handbook*

Pacemakers

If the person is to be cremated and has a pacemaker it must be removed, by a doctor or funeral director, or it could blow up the cremator.

Transporting a body

It is perfectly legal to take the body yourself from the hospital to home as long as the body is covered. Here are a few more guidelines:

✳ If the person died in hospital, a nurse must sign a release form stating you are doing your own undertaking (although this is not a legal requirement).

✳ If the body is to be picked up from the hospital mortuary, you should arrange a time and ask how many people you will need and if you need to bring anything to cover the body. (Remember this is not the public face of death, hospital mortuaries are simple and stark, and morticians are not trained to deal with grieving relatives.)

✳ Mortuary staff, because of fairly recent health and safety regulations, are not allowed to help you carry the body or place it in a coffin. However, there will usually be a trolley that you can use. You will need at least two people.

✳ Use a sufficiently large car, and bring in the coffin or shroud you have chosen. A blanket or body bag can also be used and strapped onto a stretcher.

✳ If you are taking the coffin, the Natural Death Centre recommends using broom handles to slide the coffin in and out of the car if it is very heavy.

✳ If you cannot get a big enough car, you can hire a hearse and bearers, or ask your local funeral director to help. Alternatively you can hire a van.

✳ It takes four to six people to carry a coffin. Make sure the handles on the coffin are not just for decoration.

A funeral checklist

* Obtain the cause of death certificate

* Decide whether to use a funeral director; if so, assign one

* Decide on burial or cremation

* Look at burial sites and/or crematoria

* Register the death

* Check availability for the cremation or burial as soon as possible, and book it when you can

The Medical Certificate (Certificate for the Cause of Death)

Death at home

When a person dies at home the family doctor should be informed. They will complete the medical certificate, without charge. This will be in a sealed envelope addressed to the registrar. They will also give you a formal notice stating that it has been signed.

If cremation is intended, the signature of two doctors who have viewed the body is required, for *Cremation Forms B and C*, available free from the crematorium. The doctors charge a fee of £130. If you are not using a funeral director you will have to pay these fees direct.

Death in hospital

A doctor will fill in the medical certificate as a matter of course. If cremation is intended the hospital will arrange the completion of *Cremation Forms B and C*. These forms are not required if a coroner is involved.

Registering a death

When?

Legally, the death must be registered within five days of it occurring. This period may be extended if there are extenuating circumstances, and if the coroner has been consulted.

Where?

Except in Scotland, a death can only be registered in the registration district in which the death occurred. If going to a different office, you can make a 'death by declaration': the registrar records the information and passes it on to the relevant registrar. This process will take longer. To find the relevant registrar, check with your local council.

Who?

The death must be registered by one of the following:

✳ A relative, usually the closest one

✳ An official from the hospital or nursing home

✳ An occupant of the house

✳ Someone who was present at the death

✳ Someone who is making the funeral arrangements with the funeral directors

✳ The person who found the body

✳ In Scotland, a legal representative

Most deaths are registered by a relative. The registrar would normally only allow someone else to do so if there are no relatives available.

Registering the death will normally take about half an hour. It is important to make an appointment first.

Documents you must take

The Medical Certificate of the cause of death (signed by a doctor)

Documents it's helpful but not essential to take

* The deceased's NHS medical card

* Any pension book, certificate or document relating to any pension or state benefits that the deceased was receiving

* The deceased's passport, birth certificate and marriage certificate

What you will need to know

* The date and place of death

* Date and place of birth, full names and maiden names

* Usual address and occupation

* Whether the deceased was receiving a state pension or allowance

* Name, date of birth, and occupation of surviving spouse

* Full name and occupation of father

What the registrar will give you

* A free social security form to ensure that benefits are being paid correctly

* A free certificate for Order for Burial or Cremation: the

'Green Form' (in Scotland a Certificate of Registration of Death)

✳ The registrar will advise you over any further certificate copies you require and the cost involved. These are necessary for banks, pensions and probate. It is a good idea to buy a few now because they are more expensive to buy later.

Registering stillbirths

In England and Wales, stillbirths must be registered within 42 days and not more than three months after the birth. This can be done at the hospital or the register office. For more information log on to the General Register Office website *www.gro.gov.uk* or contact your local office.

The coroner

It is the duty of the coroner to investigate any sudden, unnatural or unexplained deaths. The doctor may report a death to the coroner if the death:

✳ Has been caused by an accident or injury

✳ Has been caused by an industrial disease

✳ Happened during a surgical operation

✳ Happened before recovering from an anaesthetic

✳ Is from an unknown cause

✳ Was sudden and explained

A coroner will be notified if no doctor has attended the person for some time (14 days in England, Scotland and Wales, 28 days in Northern Ireland).

The coroner will decide whether to hold a post mortem and/or an inquest. The coroner will then notify the registrar that the death can be registered. The person registering the death will need to visit the registrar to do this. The coroner's office will keep this person informed about what to do. As these arrangements may cause delay, you should not arrange the funeral until authorized by the coroner's officer.

If a death is referred to the coroner, he or she will issue the relevant form for burial or cremation (the pink form) without charge.

If a person dies in hospital you can refuse permission for a post mortem to establish the cause of death. However, if there are unusual circumstances about the death the coroner may insist on a post mortem, and will have to issue a certificate as to the cause of death. An interim certificate can be issued to the executors of the will if an inquest is necessary.

If the coroner decides to investigate the death they may either order a post mortem examination or open an inquest on the deceased person. Once the coroner is satisfied that further examination of the body is not required they will issue a certificate called *Form E* which takes the place of the previously mentioned cremation *Forms B and C.* This form is free.

Arranging a burial

Provisional booking

When you book a burial you will need to know details about the deceased, the time and date of the funeral, the size of the coffin, and the religion, should any special provisions needs to be made. If you already have rights to a grave, the number will be required.

Notice of burial

A formal notification of the burial must be delivered to the burial authority as soon as possible. It is issued free of charge, by post if requested, from the cemetery or burial ground. The completed form is regarded as a binding contract over the work and costs involved.

Certificate of Burial or Cremation

The Notice of Burial should be accompanied by a Registrar's Certificate known as a *Green Form* (or, if referred to a coroner, the *Coroner's Order for Burial*). Some authorities may accept the order or certificate when the funeral arrives at the cemetery. The funeral cannot proceed until a certificate or order is given to the burial authority.

After the burial

The Burial Register

The cemetery staff will record the burial in the register. An entry will also be made in the Record of Graves alongside the appropriate grave number. An entry for a new grave will be made in the Register of Grants, recording the purchase of the Right of Burial and the period that this covers. A Grant of Right of Burial will be prepared and posted to the grave purchaser.

The Registrar's Certificate

Within 96 hours of the burial, the detachable portion of the Grant of Right of Burial must be sent by the cemetery registrar to the Registrar of Births, Deaths and Marriages indicating the date and place of burial.

Arranging a cremation

Because cremation destroys the body, the procedure is more complicated than for burial.

Notice of cremation

This form provides notice of the cremation and forms a binding contract regarding the payment of fees to the cremation authority. The form contains the date and time of the funeral, information about the deceased, the coffin, the service, and what is to happen to the cremated remains.

Application for cremation (Form A)

This is a statutory form issued by the crematorium or funeral director. It must be completed by the executor or nearest surviving relative and countersigned by a householder known to the applicant. The details required are quite straightforward although the applicant must state that they have no reason to object to the cremation going ahead.

Medical Forms B, C and F

These are statutory forms, with *Forms B and C* being subject to a payment upon completion to the doctors involved. *Form B* is completed by the doctor who attended the deceased before death and *Form C* by a doctor who confirms the cause of death. If the death was referred to the coroner these two certificates are not needed and you will be given *Form E*, which is free.

Questions will also be asked about whether radioactive implants or a cardiac pacemaker are present in the body, as these must be removed before cremation.

Form F is completed by a doctor appointed as the medical referee to the Cremation Authority. He or she will sign the form, if satisfied that the details on *Forms B and C* are correct. The cremation will only take place after this form has been signed.

Forms A, B and C must be submitted to the crematorium office together with the Certificate of Burial or Cremation issued by the registrar.

Burial or cremation of babies

Hospitals arrange for babies that are stillborn (after the 24th week of pregnancy), or babies that have died soon after birth, to be buried or cremated if the baby died more than 24 weeks into the pregnancy. The hospital will usually designate which method is to be used, although the parents are free to make their own arrangements.

Burial A funeral director is contracted and a specific cemetery used. There will often be a special area designated for the very young. The baby will usually be placed in a small white coffin.

Cremation A service is usually conducted for the parents who lost babies in that month.

These arrangements are free. However, parents may wish to make their own arrangements. It is sensible to consider their own death, and whether they would like to be near the baby.

Burial on private land

Burial authorisation

In England, Wales and Scotland, a free burial authorisation must be obtained before the burial takes place. Registrars of births and deaths issue 'green forms' for burial to take place. These are not issued if an inquest will be held. Instead the coroner issues a 'burial order'. Burial on private land is of no legal concern to registrars or coroners.

In England and Wales both types of burial authorisation have tear-off slips. They must be completed by the land owner or land manager, giving the date and place of burial, and must be received by the Registrar of Births and Deaths (in the area where the death occurred) within 96 hours of the burial.

Burial Register

There must be a burial register for all graves in England & Wales. For a private burial, you will need to make a Burial Register yourself. This is a document detailing the Burial. It should be treated as any important document, and made on strong paper, and kept in a safe and accessible place.

As well as a plan of the location, you must record the following details:

* if a CoE minister conducts the funeral, their name, the relevant CoE diocese and local authority parish

* name and address of the landowner

* name and address of the property

* full name of the person who is buried, along with previous names or additional names

* date of birth

* date of death

* date of burial

* address where they died

* address where they lived

✳ Ordnance Survey grid reference for the grave

✳ Land Registry reference number if the land is registered

✳ burial authorisation details

✳ entry number in the register

✳ grave number

✳ numerous ('triangulated') measurements, so the exact position of the grave can be found in future years

✳ site plan grid reading to locate the grave, which is read in the same way as an Ordnance Survey grid reference

✳ angle of the grave, showing which way the head and feet are pointing

✳ name of the person responsible for arranging the burial, such as a relative or executor of the person's Will

✳ signature, name and status of the person signing the register

✳ date when the register is signed

If there is no money – the government's Social Fund

Who?

To qualify you must:

∗ Be responsible for paying for the funeral – perhaps a spouse, or close relative if there is no spouse. If you are a friend, it must be shown that there is *no one else* who can pay.

∗ Be in receipt of certain qualifying benefits or tax credits.

What?

∗ The fund covers all the costs of a simple, respectful, low-cost funeral.

∗ The money must be paid back from the estate of the deceased if it is possible.

When?

You can claim a Funeral Payment from the date of death and up to three months after the date of the funeral. Funeral Payments are usually made in the funeral director's name.

How?

See leaflet *SB16, A Guide to the Social Fund, form SF200* from your JobCentre or social security office.

War pensioners

In certain circumstances war pensioners are entitled to their funeral being paid for from the Social Fund. In these cases it does not have to be repaid. See *WPA Leaflet 1, Notes about War Disablement and War Widow's Pensions,* or phone the veterans' free helpline on 0800 169 227.

Complaints

To complain about a funeral director contact the National Association of Funeral Directors, The Funeral Standards Council, the Society of Allied and Independent Funeral Directors, or the Trading Standards Officer at your local council.

Repatriation

If someone dies abroad, and you wish to bring the body home, a funeral director must be assigned. There are specialist companies for this process. The body must be placed in a zinc-lined coffin that is hermetically sealed, and a Certificate of Sanitisation completed. It is usual to embalm the body. If the flight is within the UK, the zinc-lined coffin is not a requirement.

Announcing a death

∗ A member of the family should announce the death as soon as possible to the key people in that person's life. It would be awful to learn of a death second-hand.

∗ A letter or card should be sent informing everyone of the funeral arrangements. You may want to specify whether flowers would be appropriate.

∗ A notice in the paper may be appropriate.

Who to inform of a death

Here's a checklist of people and organisations who may need to know:

∗ relatives and friends

∗ employer

∗ school

∗ solicitor/accountant

∗ the deceased's tax office

∗ National Insurance Contributions Office if they were self-employed (to cancel payments)

∗ Child Benefit Office (at latest within eight weeks)

✳ landlord or local authority if the deceased rented their property

✳ local authority if the deceased paid council tax, had a parking permit, was issued with a blue badge for disabled parking, or received social services help, attended day care or similar

✳ any private organisation/agency providing home help

✳ general insurance companies – contents, car, travel, medical and so on (if the deceased was the first named on an insurance policy, make contact as early as possible to check that you are still insured)

✳ pension providers/life insurance companies

✳ bank/building society

✳ mortgage provider

✳ hire purchase or loan companies

✳ credit card providers/store cards

✳ utility companies if accounts were in the deceased's name

✳ TV/internet companies with which the deceased had subscriptions

✳ any other company with which the deceased may have had rental, hire purchase or loan agreements

✳ Royal Mail, if mail needs redirecting

✳ Bereavement Register and Deceased Preference Service to remove the deceased's name from mailing lists and databases

✳ UK Passport Agency, to return and cancel a passport

✳ DVLA, to return any driving licence, cancel car tax or elicit a refund

✳ car registration documents/change of ownership

✳ clubs, trade unions, associations with seasonal membership for cancellation and refunds

✳ church/regular place of worship

✳ social groups to which the deceased belonged

✳ dentist

✳ creditors – anyone to whom the deceased owed money

✳ debtors – anyone who owed the deceased money

See *What to do after a death* on **www.direct.gov.uk** for more information and relevant numbers and procedures.

CHAPTER 10

The cost of a funeral

The costs of funerals vary widely according to what you want and what you can afford, but here is a general ballpark guide to what you can expect to pay for the various different components you might choose.

Funeral Directors

Costs can vary by a 100 per cent, so it's a good idea to ask a friend to get some quotes for you, and helpful if they are itemised and in writing (though you may have to be persistent).

∗ All Funeral directors should offer a 'simple funeral service'.

∗ A basic funeral costs between £450 – £1500.

∗ This does not include 'disbursements': the ministers fee, cremation or burial fee, doctors certificate.

* Some funeral directors will provide transport, charging mileage with a minimum charge of £50 - £80.

* Some will provide just cold storage of the body for £5-£15 a day.

The cost of burial

* The fee for a funeral service in a church is just under £100.

* A burial in a churchyard following on from a service in church is around £170.

* Burial in a churchyard on a separate occasion is around £200.

* These do not include music.

Graves

* Graves can cost from £300 to £3,000 depending on the area.

Natural Burials

* A natural burial plot costs in the region of £500 – £800.

Cremation Fees

* Creamtion fees vary from £200 -£600.

Humanist Officiant

✳ This should cost around £100 – 130

Coffins

✳ Cardboard coffins start at under £100

✳ Untreated pine coffins are around £250

✳ Bamboo coffins cost about £350 – £400

✳ Banana leaf coffin: £550 – £600

✳ Somerset willow coffin: £850

✳ Cheaper willow coffins are about £550

✳ Traditional chipboard, and veneer coffins cost between £250 - £400 (be warned these are the hardest to buy without a funeral director)

✳ Solid oak will cost you around £800

✳ Artist designed eco coffins cost from £600 - £800

Shrouds

✳ These cost from £200 for a kit to £900 for a handmade felt artist-designed shroud.

Urns

✳ A simple urn will cost around £30

✳ Papier maché urns are in the region of £40

✳ Willow and Bamboo urns cost about £45

✳ You can pay up to £150 for ceramic artist-designed urns

Memorials

✳ These can range from around £80-£200 for a plaque, to several thousand for a gravestone.

✳ £1,000 seems to be the minimum completed price for a traditional stone grave marker.

✳ Memorials for Artists start at about £1,800 for their unique commissions.

✳ You can dedicate a tree with the Woodland Trust for £10.

Conclusion

Life moves so fast. I wonder where is our ritual? Where are our Gods, on the billboards 40 feet tall, is this what we mean by immortality? We chase youth like a butterflies' dance. When did we make an enemy out of time, when did we hang onto our imaginings of youth and forget that death is in the next room?

I walk off the street into the cathedral; it's Friday at 6pm. I listen to Evensong, sunbeams light up the dust and it's beautiful, there are three other people and me. Listen, I'm as confused as you. When I was six churches terrified me, and they still do, but some things speak to your soul.

I began this process looking for answers. I thought I would plan my own funeral. I find myself sitting at my kitchen table, wondering should I really be asking my loved ones to scatter my ashes from a Buddhist temple in Northern India, far in the inaccessible Himalayas. The view is amazing, just breathtaking, but am I over thinking this? After all I went there not because I was a Buddhist, but because it rained. It rained for the first time in 16 years in those mountains and there was nowhere else to go. I learned a lot, but that was then. That was my adventure.

This funeral isn't for me, after all. I am dead. The funeral is for them. The living. Surely they will know. They will do what they have to, what they can do. They will take me to a place I loved, and think of me. That's all anyone can ever do. They will also know that if the music is rubbish I will haunt them.

I still lie awake at night trying to grasp the notion of eternity. And it is still unfathomable. I just try to wonder instead of fear. All we can do is to celebrate the adventures of those we have lost, and find the courage to let them go, with honesty, with love.

I hope this book helps.

> *"We deal with death – the idea of the thing – by dealing with our dead, the thing itself. So whatever we do to accompany our dead to whatever the next thing is, the further shore or the heaven, the valhalla or the void, or the oblivion... it's our obligation I think to take them there, to take them at least to the edge of it, whether the edge is a fire or a tomb. Wherever we take them we should go*

there with them and say, 'Now you go there, I go back to life'. Whether or not you do that in a religious context, that's a deeply human thing."

Thomas Lynch

"If you got a chance, if you stormed the main stage, and grabbed the microphone just before the bouncers dragged you off and kicked the shit out of you, and you got to shout one word, just one at the mass, It would have to be LOVE.

"And that's all you can do at a funeral. I know it hurts but...love."

Rupert Callender

Useful contacts

We've put together a list of useful organisations to contact which are referred to in this book. As contact details often change we've put the list on our website where we can update it regularly, rather than printed it here. You can find the list at www.whiteladderpress.com; click on 'useful contacts' next to the information about this book.

If you don't have access to the Internet you can contact White Ladder Press by any of the means listed on the next page and we'll print off a hard copy and post it to you free of charge.

Contact us

You're welcome to contact White Ladder Press if you have any questions or comments for either us or the author. Please use whichever of the following routes suits you.

Phone 01803 813343 between 9am and 5.30pm

Email enquiries@whiteladderpress.com

Fax 01803 813928

Address White Ladder Press, Great Ambrook, Near Ipplepen, Devon TQ12 5UL

Website www.whiteladderpress.com

What can our website do for you?

If you want more information about any of our books, you'll find it at *www.whiteladderpress.com*. In particular you'll find extracts from each of our books, and reviews of those that are already published. We also run special offers on future titles if you order online before publication. And you can request a copy of our free catalogue.

Many of our books also have links pages, useful addresses and so on relevant to the subject of the book. You'll also find out a bit more about us and, if you're a writer yourself, you'll find our submission guidelines for authors. So please check us out and let us know if you have any comments, questions or suggestions.